A BIG ASK

The Story of Ford's Triumphant Return to Le Mans

David Phillips

Kenya –
Thanks for all you do
for the team

To Mary for your humor, unwavering love and support.
I bless the day I found you.

© 2016 by David Phillips
Print ISBN: 978-1-48358-568-0
eBook ISBN: 978-1-48358-567-3

Photography credits:

Corvette/Richard Price (16), Michael Levitt (27, 66),
Multimatic (30, 32, 157, 161), Mike Hull (36), Roush Yates
Engines (112, 113), Michelin/Rick Dole (116, 118, 130, 176,
194, 196), Kevin Kennedy (123), Chip Ganassi Racing (151,
158), David Phillips (155). Ford Motor Company/Dominic
James (2, 3, 9, 134, 135, 140, 143, 148), Brecht Decanc (12,
92, 93, 171, 180), Wes Duenkel (15, 48, 49, 61, 72, 77, 79, 81,
85, 86, 87, 102, 117, 189, 191), Bob Chapman (65, 82, 96, 99,
101, 193) and Nick Dugan (182). Cover photographs and all
other photography courtesy of Ford/Drew Gibson.

Cover Design and Layout by Matthew Phillips

"For any engineering team, any race team to come in your first year and have an expectation you're going to win the biggest race of the year…it's a big ask."

—Raj Nair
Executive Vice President, Product Development and
Chief Technical Officer, Ford Motor Company

FOREWORD

IN THE SPRING OF 2015, the rumor mill in the automobile world started buzzing. And it kept buzzing, until the buzz got so loud it was as piercing as the crackle of a V6 racing engine. The rumor started to feel like the worst kept secret in the Motor City, all anyone in automotive circles in America wanted to talk about. But was it true? No way! Couldn't be...

Ford Motor Company was going to build a new racing car and go roaring back to Le Mans, on the 50th anniversary of the company's historic victory at the 24-hour classic, in 1966.

When Dearborn finally made the announcement on June 12, 2015, it still felt too good to be true. An all-new Ford GT road car and race car. Two factory-backed race teams—one to compete in the FIA World Endurance Championship and the other in the IMSA WeatherTech SportsCar Championship. The Rolex 24 at Daytona. The 12 Hours of Sebring. Spa-Francorchamps, the Nürburgring, the Circuit of the Americas. And, of course, the most challenging and important motor race in the world: The 24 Hours of Le Mans. The pictures of the car revealed that day—painted red, white, and blue—proved breathtaking, beautiful, fearsome, and American as all hell. One glance was enough to get the engine in your ribcage throttling.

This story begins over 50 years ago. Henry Ford II—the grandson of Ford's founder and arguably the most powerful chief executive of his day—got tangled in a business deal gone bad. A rivalry resulted between Henry II of Dearborn, Michigan, and Enzo Ferrari of Modena, Italy. These were walking legends in the auto business who made eponymous cars that defined their respective nations. The rivalry between them played out at the 24 Hours of Le Mans starting in 1964, and this war of speed is today considered the Golden Age of Motor Racing. Never had such beautiful cars traveled so fast. Never had so much been at stake in car racing. It remains one of the greatest grudge matches not just in racing history, but in all of sporting history.

As readers likely know, Ford Motor Company defeated Ferrari Le Mans in 1966. That checkered flag can be defined as the most important victory in the annals of American racing. So for Ford to announce an all new GT racer, and an all-new campaign to win Le Mans in the GT class would be the story of the year. Back in the 1960s, icons like Carroll Shelby and Henry Ford II were behind the effort. This time around, it would be Edsel B. Ford II, Bill Ford, Henry Ford III, Mark Fields, Raj Nair, Chip Ganassi and Larry Holt…among many others.

You have to hand it to a bunch of guys who decide to put their famed motor company's legacy and reputation on the line on the biggest stage of them all. The new Ford GT would be competing against Ferraris, Porsches, Aston Martins and perhaps most exciting of all, Ford's crosstown rivals—the Corvettes of Chevrolet.

The stage was set, but nobody could have predicted what would happen next. And that is the story you are about to read. It's a story of heroes, danger, and speed. It's a story that would have made old Henry Ford himself very proud.

—A.J. Baime
Author of
Go Like Hell: Ford, Ferrari, and Their Battle for Speed and Glory at Le Mans

Circuit de la Sarthe   Length: 8.4667 Miles (13.6259km)

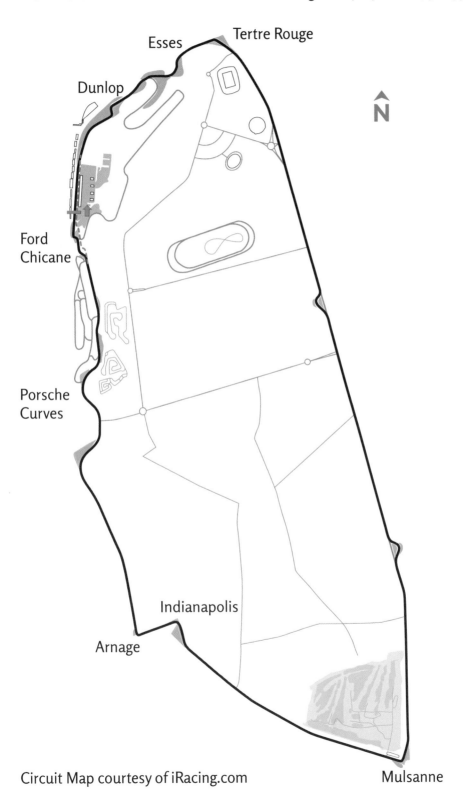

Tertre Rouge

Esses

Dunlop

N̂

Ford
Chicane

Porsche
Curves

Indianapolis

Arnage

Mulsanne

Chapter 1
Beginnings

GENESIS AND THE BIG BANG ASIDE, events, human endeavors and ideas seldom have a definitive beginning.

Did World War I begin with the assassination of Archduke Ferdinand at 11 a.m. on June 28, 1914? When Germany declared war on Russia and France six weeks later? Or with the formation of the Triple Alliance in 1882?

When did NASA's Apollo program originate? On May 25, 1961 when President Kennedy announced the goal of sending an American safely to the Moon and back by decade's end? When Orville Wright took flight in Kitty Hawk? Or when Paleo Man's gaze first fixed on that ivory orb in a sky unsullied by light pollution?

And when was rock 'n roll born? With the release of *Rock Around the Clock* or *My Man Rocks Me (With One Steady Roll)*? With gospel, R&B, boogie-woogie, rockabilly or jump blues? With Bill Haley and the Comets? Alan Freed? Chuck Berry? Howlin' Wolf? Elvis? Jelly Roll Morton? Fats Domino? Carl Perkins? Ike Turner?

Beginnings, it seems, are in the eye of the beholder. Indeed, for more than a generation the great flashpoint of American politics has been the question of when life itself begins.

So to point to a definitive moment when The Ford Motor Company set out to re-capture the glory of its most fabled international motorsports triumph—a 1-2-3 finish in the 1966 24 Hours of Le Mans, the first of four consecutive victories—is nothing if not an exercise in subjectivity. Better to explore the roots of Ford's Le Mans reprise in the minds of some of the principle characters spearheading and contributing to the effort.

Of one thing we can be certain: Henry Ford II's fascination with the 24 Hours of Le Mans—in fact, an obsession that spurred his bid to acquire Ferrari in the early '60s and, when he was rebuffed, to spend untold millions to win "La Ronde Infernale" courses through the veins of his company and heirs to this day.

"My real grandfather died when I was seven," explains Henry Ford III, Ford Performance Marketing Manager, "so my early consciousness of Le Mans was more wrapped-up in Carroll Shelby. Not just for me, but for a lot of Americans, he was Le Mans. What he orchestrated with Ford at Le Mans is certainly part of the family DNA.

"After college, I was working at Galpin Ford in LA when Carroll arranged to meet for dinner. The first words he ever spoke to me were 'Your grandfather was a son-of-a-bitch.'"

Although many might have retorted, "it takes one to know one," the fact remains that Ford formed a familial bond with the Le Mans-winning driver who was destined to mastermind the 1966 triumph (not to mention father the Shelby Cobra and Shelby Mustang); a bond so close that Ford refers to Shelby as his "de facto grandfather."

One would be hard-pressed to find a man who bears less of a physical resemblance to the forbidding Henry Ford II or

Edsel B. Ford II, Henry Ford III and 1966 Le Mans-winning Ford GT40

Raj Nair

larger-than-life Carroll Shelby than Raj Nair. But as Ford's Executive Vice President, Product Development and Chief Technical Officer, the jockey-sized Nair is every bit the father of the EcoBoost Ford GT as The Deuce and Shelby were of the Ford GT40.

The son of India-born college professors, Nair was not exactly born to a household keen on, let alone obsessed with, motorsports. However, from his earliest days the St. Louis native was a car guy and that passion eventually led him to race Formula Fords and, later, in the Skip Barber Racing Series.

"There's a certain feeling that can only be experienced racing wheel-to-wheel, both man and machine at their absolute limits," says Nair. "I've since come to enjoy racing on three levels: as a driver competing on the track, as an engineer appreciating the incredible innovation required for success and, of course, as a fan."

But it was a fourth perspective—as an automotive executive who abhors the status quo—that drove Nair to formulate Ford's return to Le Mans and, with the backing of Ford CEO Mark

Fields, champion the program to Ford's Board of Directors, opting to develop a 21st century Ford GT for the Le Mans GTE-Pro class rather than going for the overall win in the esoteric and astronomically expensive LMP1 class or building a GTE-Pro class super-Mustang with but a passing resemblance to its namesake. At the same time, Nair launched a thorough revamp—termed a rebirth in some quarters—of Ford's motorsports programs corresponding with a newly aggressive line of high-performance road cars under the "Ford Performance" rubric.

Quick-witted and gregarious, it's hard to imagine anyone calling Nair a "son of a bitch"—although nobody climbs the corporate ladder from a body and assembly operations engineer to director of new model programs, Advanced and Manufacturing Engineering, Vehicle Operations at Ford in a dozen years without sharp elbows.

Not so Chip Ganassi. The son a WWII veteran who made a fortune in the Western Pennsylvania construction industry was a race driver short on patience and long on talent, out-qualifying fellow rookies Bobby Rahal, Danny Sullivan and Hurley Haywood in the 1982 Indy 500 and earning the STP Most Improved IndyCar Driver award the following season. Ganassi, who still owns a Ford GT40 slot car he raced as a youth, stepped away from the cockpit after competing in the 1987 24 Hours of Le Mans to build "the kind of team I would have wanted to drive for."

Success was not instantaneous. But as he stocked his organization with a potent brew of seasoned veterans, up 'n comers and "first adopters" including managing director, Mike Hull, Ganassi matured into a kinder, gentler but still fiercely competitive team owner; one who demands excellence of his employees but treats them like his extended family; one whose vocabulary does not include the phrase "that's good enough" and whose team has earned 17 series championships and more than 160 race wins including four Indianapolis 500s, the Daytona 500, Brickyard 400, a half dozen Rolex 24s at Daytona and the 12 Hours of Sebring…at last count.

Indeed, among his contemporary team owners, only Roger Penske's statistics compare with those of Ganassi who, to be fair, was still *driving* race cars when Penske Racing captured its sixth Indy 500. While the two enjoy a personal friendship and mutual respect, only those close to Ganassi appreciate how much he enjoyed snatching the 2015 IndyCar title from Penske's

Chip Ganassi

grasp in the final laps of the final race of the season…or what it would mean to him to be the first of the two to occupy the top step of the podium at Le Mans.

Just as Ford called on the racing expertise of Shelby's team (together with rival squads Holman Moody, Alan Mann and John Wyer Racing) to achieve its Le Mans success in the 1960s, so Ford partnered with Ganassi and his organization to campaign the EcoBoost Ford GT. The partners were hardly strangers. Having captured a pair of 24 Hours of Daytona and Daytona Prototype (DP) series championships with BMW power and a team of drivers including Joey Hand and Scott Pruett, Ganassi joined forces with the Blue Oval in 2014 to campaign a Riley chassis powered by Ford's 3.5 liter, turbocharged V6—aka the EcoBoost—taking five wins in two seasons including the 24 Hours of Daytona and 12 Hours of Sebring.

"We watched Chip's organization for a while and saw what his organization did in DP as our partner," says Nair. "Obviously his organization has enjoyed a tremendous amount of success. When we decided to up our game in preparation for the Ford

GT program we wanted the best, and it would be hard to say in IMSA DP that Ganassi is not the best. So as we started the discussions the cultures fit and the personalities fit...maybe fit a little too much!

"I'm not going to say we had this grand plan written down where the end game was 2016 Le Mans, we'll do a production Ford GT with the EcoBoost engine therefore we'll need to put the EcoBoost in a DP and race it with Chip," he continues. "Having said that, certainly in my mind it was 'If we're going to do that, then we'd better have this step now...this is a real opportunity in 2016. But if we're going to do it, then we have to lay some groundwork right now. If we don't do it, the groundwork is still great. But if we're going to do it with a new car and a new engine, let's have some things stable, including the organization we're partnering with.'"

Chip Ganassi Racing achieved considerable success with BMW, but the Bavarian automaker never truly seemed to embrace the Daytona Prototype program; didn't give it much credence internally or leverage the success publically. Committed to moving forward with the team's sports car racing program, Ganassi followed up when Pruett (who counts Edsel B. Ford II as a personal friend) told him of Ford's interest in ramping-up its Daytona Prototype program.

"We made a switch over to Ford in DP, really not knowing there was some big carrot out there at the end of the stick, but wanting to stay in sports car and knowing we would be involved in developing this EcoBoost engine for Ford Racing," says Ganassi. "We said: 'That sounds like fun' and that's what we did."

Although there was no agenda, covert or otherwise, about a Ford GT project or Le Mans underlying the Daytona Prototype partnership, it wasn't long before Ganassi heard whispers of another, more ambitious program in the works at Ford. Nair suggested the Ganassi brain trust come to Detroit for a look-see as early as 2014, but it was months before Ganassi and Hull paid what proved to be a consequential visit to Dearborn, where they were introduced to the top secret "Project Phoenix," now known as the Ford GT.

Like virtually everyone seeing the car for the first time, they were impressed—to put it mildly. Visceral reactions aside, however, having grown accustomed to competing in the rigidly controlled technical environments of contemporary NASCAR,

IndyCar racing and even the Daytona Prototype class, Ganassi and Hull were intrigued by the prospect of developing an exciting new car in a motorsports arena that embraces engineering innovation and development.

"At the end of the day, the Ford GT has four tires, a steering wheel and you have to shift gears," Ganassi says, "but it's got some nice enhancements and technologies we could sink our teeth into. That really energized us and rejuvenated some of those brain cells that got us into racing in the first place.

"At that time I don't think we realized how much the tradition and a lot of the foundations of Ford itself are in this program; the same ones that were in the original Ford GT; that, not only within Ford, but how the underpinnings of so much of racing today go back to the Ford GT; not just the reasons to go racing, but the technology, the personnel, the diversity of the team itself. All those underpinnings go back to the '60s when the modern era of Ford motor racing began."

The program would be nothing if not ambitious. In addition to Ganassi's sports car team racing Ford GTs in the International Motor Sports Association's (IMSA) WeatherTech SportsCar

Larry Holt

Championship in North America, Toronto-based automotive engineering and manufacturing giant Multimatic was contracted to build both the racing and road going versions of the Ford GT and to open a second racing front in the *Fédération Internationale de l'Automobile*'s (FIA) World Endurance Championship (WEC) under the Ford Chip Ganassi Racing banner from a base in England. If all went according to plan, the two programs would unite for a four-car effort in the 24 Hours of Le Mans.

In contrast to its relatively new partnership with Ganassi, Ford's relationship with Multimatic is as extensive as it is long-lived. As well as working with Dearborn on the development of a host of road cars, Multimatic has raced a variety of Fords throughout North America since the early '90s, winning the inaugural Daytona Prototype race at the 24 Hours of Daytona in 2002 in a Ford-powered car of their own design.

Outside of knowledgeable racing circles, however, Larry Holt is not likely to be mentioned in the same breath as Roger Penske or Chip Ganassi. But make no mistake: In terms of accomplishments and influence on the North American motorsports scene, Multimatic's Vice President of Engineering runs second to nobody. A doppelganger of *Back to the Future*'s Emit "Doc" Brown, Holt is the lynchpin to a Multimatic motorsport program that counts among its successes class wins in the 12 Hours of Sebring, the 24 Hours of Daytona and, yes, the 24 Hours of Le Mans.

"My father was a big motor racing guy," says Holt. "He had a huge collection of books, a lot of sports car stuff and, as a kid I would read these books and learn about Le Mans.

"Then my first Scalectrix set had an Austin-Healey and a Mercedes...Kind of weird, really, to have a Scalectrix set around that horrible accident in 1955," he says, referring to what is often called racing's darkest hour, when 83 people died when a car plunged into the crowd at Le Mans.

"So I had this whole understanding of Le Mans. I remember the Ford win and what a big deal that was. Then in the '90s we began doing a lot of carbon fiber body and damper work for the Dodge Viper program, and started coming to Le Mans in '97, '98 and '99. The first time I ever came to Le Mans as a competitor was in 2000 with the B2K40 Lola. We came basically with no spares, no money...and we won. I thought: 'Shit. This is not so difficult.' Then I came back six or seven times after that and got my ass kicked.

"So I've been there a lot of times and said: 'I ain't fuckin' coming back,'" he continues. "It's a very difficult race, it really is. And then you get a different deal and you come back and it's all magical again. And it is—it really is a magical place."

If Ford, Ganassi and Multimatic had an ace in the proverbial hole, it was George Howard-Chappell. The lanky, authoritative Englishman brought an impeccable resume to the EcoBoost Ford GT program—one rooted in the hugely competitive British Touring Car Championship, a stay at the Lotus Formula One team and highlighted by class wins at Le Mans with two of sports car racing's most iconic marques—Ferrari and Aston Martin— as technical director and team principal at the ProDrive team.

Inevitably, Howard-Chappell had worked with Multimatic during his time at ProDrive and when he resigned that position, Holt began courting him to join Multimatic as director of its motorsports program. When Howard-Chappell accepted the offer in early 2013, Ford's return to Le Mans (and Multimatic's role in it) was far from assured. But when the Ford GT—and Multimatic's partnership in the program—got the green light, Holt immediately re-assigned Howard-Chappell as project director of the Ford GT. What's more, he would also assume

Dave Pericak

the role of team manager of the "second" prong of the Ford Chip Ganassi Racing team, Multimatic's WEC program.

As with many of his new teammates, Le Mans holds a very special place of honor in Howard-Chappell's psyche.

"Whenever people ask about the highlights from my time in racing," he explained to *Motor Sport*'s Simon Arron, "I never mention F1. The answer always seems to be 'Le Mans.'"

You might say the feeling is mutual.

"When we met with FIA and the *Automobile Club de l'Ouest* (organizer of the 24 Hours of Le Mans), telling them we were thinking about this program, we had George next to us. They said: 'You've got the right guy,'" recalls Dave Pericak, the long-time chief engineer of the Mustang who Nair tapped to lead the company's unified spectrum of high-performance programs as director of Ford Performance. "When you have the head of the sanctioning bodies tell you you've picked the right guy to run your program, that's a pretty good sign."

Pericak never owned or raced a Ford GT slot car, didn't read up on the history of Le Mans in his father's library, never broke bread with Carroll Shelby, but that doesn't mean he wasn't keenly aware that Le Mans is in his company's blood. His appreciation of the event expanded exponentially when he attended the 2015 race as part of Ford's announcement of its plans to race there the following year.

"My awareness of Le Mans has been through the history of the company and what it meant to the company," he says "Never in my wildest dreams did I think I'd be leading a race team as we returned to that stage, for the Ford GT to try to repeat history.

"It's not something I always dreamt of doing but it was something I've always been aware of and now to go back… even though I'd read all about Le Mans, seen movies, videos, that kind of stuff, until you experience it live and in person you can't imagine how grandiose it is, how big the track is and how it sprawls over the landscape; the track to the people to the machines, to the build-up: It's unbelievable."

When it comes to Ford, you don't have to share the company's last name or occupy a corner office in Dearborn to appreciate the 24 Hours of Le Mans. Not unlike Holt, Ford Performance aerodynamicist Bernie Marcus won in his first visit to Le Mans as part of Kremer Racing. Of course, that was a few years ago, 1979 to be precise. Marcus grew up near Cologne and, as a teenager, went to work at Kremer polishing wheels. Racing appetite whetted, he pursued formal training in mechanical engineering, which led to him designing bodywork for Kremer's Le Mans winning Porsche.

"We were very fortunate," says Marcus. "Le Mans is a very, very difficult race; very hard to win. You have to have a fast, reliable car, good drivers, good strategy...and of course luck has to be on your side. After the race I saw Bob Wollek in the paddock. 'You are the luckiest bastard in the world!" he said. "You win your first time at Le Mans and I've been trying for years and years.'"

Among history's most accomplished sports car racers, Wollek competed in the 24 Hours of Le Mans some 30 times and never managed an overall win before he was struck and killed in 2001 by an errant motorist while riding his bicycle after a day of practice at Sebring.

Mike O'Gara never raced at Le Mans, had never even attended the race until he made a reconnaissance trip there in 2014. Of a compact frame and ready laugh (often at his own expense), O'Gara cut his racing teeth on the dirt oval tracks of the Midwest. Still, as the unflappable team manager of a Ganassi sports car program that scored four wins in two seasons with the Ford-powered Daytona Prototype—including the 2014 12 Hours of Sebring—O'Gara was keenly aware of the gravity of the 24 Hours of Le Mans even before he made a "scouting" trip to the event soon after Ford's partnership with Ganassi was announced. That awareness was duly heightened by his introduction to the event.

"There's only one thing that compares with walking into Le Mans for the first time," he says. "That's the first time you see the Indianapolis Motor Speedway: Your jaw drops. You know immediately: 'This place is very special.'"

John Hennek would second those emotions. Race engineer on the EcoBoost Daytona Prototype, he came to the Ganassi team from Adrian Fernandez Racing where he worked first on Indy cars and, later, the team's Acura LMP2 sports car. It was during the latter phase of his time with Fernandez that he got his introduction to Le Mans.

"I was always an Indy car guy," he explains. "I had this sort of tunnel vision that the racing world began and ended with Indy cars and the Indianapolis 500. Then I went to Le Mans with Adrian's LMP2 program. The first test day—I'm not even talking about the race...the first test day I walked in and said

Sebastien Bourdais

WOW!

"You can just feel the history of the place. OK, the track may not be exactly the same as it was in the '50s and '60s but it's got the same DNA. And to see the money invested in the race by teams and manufacturers…"

Sebastien Bourdais knows a thing or two about the history of Le Mans. After all, he's written some of it, having competed in the 24 Hours ten times. Although he is better known as the man who won four consecutive IndyCar titles for the team owned by Paul Newman and Carl Haas between 2004 and 2007 (to go with several wins in recent years for KVRT Racing), his name immediately surfaced as a potential driver in the Ford GT program. Why not? His Le Mans experience included a pair of runner-up finishes as a factory driver for Peugeot during the French automaker's epic battles with Audi from 2007-'09…and it never hurts to have a French driver or two on your team at Le Mans.

What's more, Sebastien Bourdais was not born just anywhere in France, but in Le Mans; and not just anywhere in Le Mans, but at the *Clinique du Tertre Rouge*, literally a stone's throw from the Tertre Rouge corner that has launched cars onto the famed Mulsanne Straightaway for nearly a century…and a well struck 3-wood away from where a contemporary of Henry Ford named Wilbur Wright made the first public demonstration flights of the Wright airplane.

Suffice to say that, while his gene sequencing may differ from that of a Henry Ford III, a Chip Ganassi, Larry Holt or George Howard-Chappell, Sebastien Bourdais has Le Mans in his DNA. In spades. And yet, it took him some years to understand that his "local" race was something quite special.

"As a kid we used to watch the practice from the enclosure between Mulsanne Corner and Indianapolis (curve)," he recalls. "It cost a couple of francs for a ticket. But to me, it was just a big event in Le Mans; I didn't really begin to understand what a huge event it is worldwide until I was in the paddock when my father competed in the race and I looked around at all the great teams, the cars, the drivers, all the nationalities represented… then I thought to myself, 'I want to win this race someday.'"

After making his mark as European F3000 champion, four-time IndyCar champion, and twice finishing second at Le Mans with Peugeot, suffice to say Sebastien Bourdais still very much

Joey Hand

wanted to win Le Mans.

So did Joey Hand, who teamed with Pruett to drive the Ford Chip Ganassi Racing Daytona Prototype in 2015, and whose youthful California patina masks the soul of a hardtack-tough racer. Once on the fast track to the Indianapolis 500, he earned a prestigious Valvoline Team USA Scholarship at age 19 before capturing the 1999 Star Mazda Series and finishing third in the 2001 Toyota Atlantic Championship. But Hand's career veered away from the Indianapolis Motor Speedway toward the Circuit de la Sarthe when he signed to drive for BMW's IMSA and, later, German Touring Car Championship teams.

Hand's big chance came in 2011 when Ganassi invited him to drive his BMW-powered Daytona Prototype in the 24 Hours of Daytona. He made the most of his chance, partnering with Pruett, Memo Rojas and Graham Rahal to earn yet another Rolex watch for their team owner.

"The first time I drove for this team, I told Chip: 'I want to drive for you full time,'" Hand recalls. "He said: 'Kid, one day you will.' And I said: 'I'm going to hold you to it.'"

Later that same year, Hand got his introduction to Le Mans when he co-drove a BMW M3 with Andy Priaulx and Dirk Müller to third place in the GTE-Pro class.

"Growing up racing go-karts then Star Mazda and Formula Atlantic, I always had my eye on Indianapolis as 'The Big One,'" says Hand, whose crash helmet is emblazoned with the names of his wife (Natalie) and children (Chase and Kaylee). "Of course I knew about Le Mans, but until you've experienced it for the first time, you have no idea how big a deal Le Mans is. There were more fans at the technical inspection the week before the race than at practically any race I'd ever done!"

As a youth, Scott Maxwell experienced his first Le Mans in the company of his father, a teacher in the Canadian armed forces stationed in Germany. Yet Maxwell never expected to race at Le Mans after his family moved home to Canada, even after he started racing—and winning—in go karts, Formula Vees and Formula Ford; even after he accepted Holt's offer to go to work for Multimatic as a test/development/race driver. And yet, he was at the wheel of Multimatic's Lola when the team won at Le Mans in Y2K. He's never forgotten it.

"I never thought I'd be driving at Le Mans…and I ended up going five times," he says. "It was not a blasé thing where I thought: 'OK Le Mans this year, Indy next year.' For me it was a big deal. And then we won. It was a race of attrition, not flat-out racing like it is now. But we kept out of trouble and at the end of the race we were in first place. And if anyone asks me what the biggest moment was in my career I'll say in a heartbeat that it was standing on the podium, looking out at the mass of people at Le Mans."

In contrast, Billy Johnson, who co-drives a Multimatic Mustang in IMSA's Continental Tire SportsCar Challenge with Maxwell, had never been to Le Mans. Yet he understood, intellectually at least, what the race means.

"Le Mans is like the Indy 500 or the Daytona 500—it's on any race driver's bucket list," says Johnson. "It's one of the races you want to win. And to have the chance to do it with Ford and all the history Ford has at Le Mans, a driver couldn't ask for more."

To put the 24 Hours of Le Mans truly into perspective, however, one could do worse—much worse—than turn to a man who would be racing at la Sarthe with the same team for the 17th consecutive year in June of 2016. That would be Doug Fehan, Corvette Racing's charismatic program manager who led the 'Vettes to class wins at Le Mans in 2001, 2002, 2004, 2005,

Scott Maxwell and Billy Johnson

Doug Fehan

2006, 2009, 2011 and 2015.

"Le Mans? She is a formidable foe who has time and history on her side. Going up against her is what I look at more than the other competitors," says Fehan, who describes racing as 'like a drug.'

"Le Mans is the most formidable foe you will face, and that goes well beyond what you will face on the race track. You're away from home for 23 days—no wife, no mom, no dad, no pet, no girlfriend. Nothing. Strange country. Different language. Different food. Wednesday 'til 2 a.m., back at 8. Thursday until 2 a.m., back at 8 on Friday. All day Friday doing those cars and trying to get in bed by midnight. Getting up Saturday at 5 a.m. to be at the track at 6. Get ready for that 9 a.m. warm-up. Then wait until 3 o'clock to start the race…and now we start a 24-hour endurance race? Are you kidding me?

"Every year people say: 'Are you confident about your Le Mans race?' and I say: 'Here's what I'm confident about: We're as well prepared as we can be this year.' And that's all you can be. To suggest otherwise is naive foolishness from someone who has not been there very often."

Chapter 2
Gestation and Birth

THE FORD GT ACTUALLY BEGAN as a Mustang…in a manner of speaking. After initially considering and dismissing the prospects of competing for the overall win at Le Mans in the LMP1 class as too expensive, risky and of minimal value to the company, Nair initially approached Multimatic about building what amounted to a GTE-Pro class Mustang on steroids to compete at Le Mans in celebration of Ford's 1966 triumph. Known as "Project Silver," the program would have produced an EcoBoost V6-powered Mustang in time for the 2015 Le Mans, providing a "buffer" year of competition to prepare for the 50th anniversary of Ford's historic 1-2-3 finish.

But there were several problems. For instance, so many liberties would have had to be taken in the design of the car to make it a competitive GTE-Pro proposition that, in Holt's words, "You'd have had to squint real hard to see a Mustang." And owing to its tenuous connections to the pony car on sale in its showrooms, Ford would have had to build 100 examples of the car (known as "homologation specials") before the WEC would have certified it to compete in a GTE-Pro class designed, in theory, for cars "having an aptitude for sport with 2 doors, 2 or 2+2 seats, opened or closed, which can be used perfectly legally on the open road and available for sale thanks to the dealer network of a manufacturer recognized by the (FIA) Endurance Committee."

Was the market really crying out for Mustangs costing a quarter-million dollars? What's more, the fact that the WEC was known to be leaning toward a more "mid-engine-friendly" rules package starting in 2016 meant the Super Mustang's best chance to win Le Mans might come in 2015 after all.

After further consideration, Nair—"the soul of the Ford Motor Company," according to *Autoweek*—hatched an alternative plan brilliant in its multi-faceted appeal. Rather than trying to fit a square peg in the round hole of GTE-Pro regulations with a Super Mustang of marginal lineage and no assurances of a return on Ford's investment on either the financial or competition side of the ledger, why not make a real statement about Ford's ability to conceive, design and deliver a super-high-performance automobile by building a worthy successor to the Ford GT40? Yes, it had been tried a decade ago with what amounted to a retro Ford GT40, but that effort had fallen short technically, aesthetically, and competition-wise (although Robertson Racing had managed a third-place finish in GTE-Am class at the 2011 Le Mans). Do it right this time and Ford might well have its cake and eat it too: a car capable of winning Le Mans *and* a highly desirable super exotic with a sticker price into the mid-six figures, thus justifying the expense of meeting the homologation requirement and at least defraying the costs of a race program whose intangible benefits would be incalculable…if all went as hoped.

With the backing of CEO Mark Fields and Chairman Bill Ford, Nair's plan for a 21st century Ford GT was approved by the Board of Directors. Now the hard work began.

In the fall of 2014 Nair began assembling a Who's Who of Ford's designers and engineers to commence work on the Ford GT, in partnership with Multimatic and in a black ops environment worthy of the CIA or MI5. Headed by Ford Vice President of Design Moray Callum, the group included Todd Willing (Chief Designer for Advanced Design), Chris Svensson, (Design Director of the Americas), Amko Leenarts, Global Director of Interior Design and Kip Ewing (Chief Engineer) and was afforded a studio deep in the bowels of the Ford design studio in Dearborn. They were charged with conceiving and designing the new Ford GT basically in their spare time—there was to be no compromising their "routine" work; nor was anyone in the Ford "mainstream" to have the slightest hint of what was afoot.

When it comes to designing a worthy successor to one of history's most iconic racecars there's bad news and good news. The bad news? It can be an intimidating undertaking, akin to painting a 21st century version of the *Mona Lisa*, sculpting a

Ford GT and Ford GT40

modern *David*, penning a contemporary *Canterbury Tales* or "updating" the *Ave Maria*. The good news? If you're marching orders are to pay homage to the original, you have starting points. In the case of the new Ford GT, one of the starting points derived from the model designation of the original Ford GT40—with "40" the key term, given that it referenced the fact that the original Ford GT was 40 inches tall at its highest point.

Beyond that, the design team's mission was to create an unmistakably modern interpretation of the Ford GT40; one whose lineage instantly hearkened to the Le Mans winners of the 1960s without being cartoonishly retro.

Crucially, the 2016 Ford GT not only owed much to the original Ford GT40 in appearance but in its bedrock design philosophy as well. Although less than 100 road-going GT40s were built and sold to the public to meet the homologation requirements of the era, the Ford GT40 was first and foremost a race car. Indeed, its shape was rooted in the Lola Mk6 that raced at la Sarthe in 1962 and '63 and that led Ford to contract with Lola's Eric Broadley to build the initial Ford GTs. The road-going version came later as, if not an afterthought, a limited

Chris Svensson

production vehicle long on show and go. Practicality? Not so much.

So Callum's team was tasked with creating a car that would win races, specifically the 24 Hours of Le Mans, in parallel with designing one of the most potent supercars anybody with a spare half million bucks burning a hole in their pocket could buy and drive on public roads. "When we started this project we already knew we were going to go racing," Svensson says. "That was one of the controlling goals that set this project in motion: to celebrate the 50th anniversary of the win by the Ford GT in the 1966 Le Mans."

Thus the performance goals were unlike those of a normal road car. The design team had extreme performance targets, and the cause and effect of creating a winning racecar enabled them simultaneously to produce a road car as stunning in performance as in appearance.

"We followed the same ethos the Ford GT40 followed: We're going to produce a car, it's going to go racing and it's going to beat the competition," Svennson says. "The fact that we created

20

a car that is beautiful…that's my job, but it's almost secondary. The three criteria were that it was to be a test bed for technologies in terms of engine development; it was supposed to really push the boundaries in terms of material usage, light weight carbon fiber, and it allowed us to really stretch our understanding of aerodynamics and deliver a car that was far superior to anything else in this segment in terms of aerodynamics.

"Even though it was something of the future, we really wanted it to have familiarity in terms of the original GT40 and have certain key design elements that were intrinsic to that form. We wanted to do a modern interpretation of them. So the shapes of the headlamps and the nostrils in the nose, the visor glass… you can draw the lines back to the original design in '65, but they're all treated in a modern and contemporary way.

"But first impressions are it jogs your memory; you pick these things up and you don't really understand why, but it's very obvious it's a Ford."

The styling cues linking the new Ford GT to the Ford GT40 came only after the basic parameters for a Le Mans-winning racing car had been developed. Square one for Svensson and his team was the fact that the new car had to be mid-engined and had to use the Ford EcoBoost turbo V6. Given those fundamentals they next looked at the highest expression of a current mid-engine GT as a starting point for the dimensional box in which

Ford GT interior

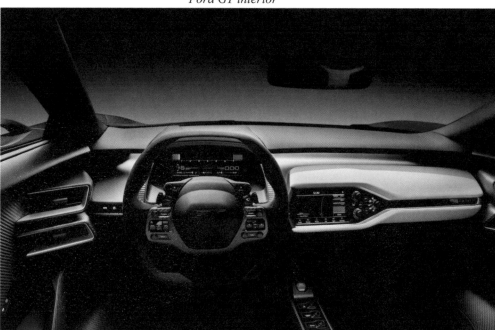

George Howard-Chappell

they would work.

"It would have been relatively easy for us to just copy the architecture and proportions of the best car in the marketplace, the Ferrari 458 Speciale," says Svensson. "But that's not what we wanted to do. We wanted a unique perspective on what we do as a company.

"The design team really thrived because we were able to do something unique. We had to tie all this together and make sure it looks pretty good, but that wasn't the main part of the program. The main part of the program was performance-driven."

Case in point, most road cars are equipped with a cross beam running from one side of the car to the other to which the dashboard is mounted. In contrast, the Ford GT's carbon fiber dashboard is a structural member of the tub. Thus the tub is not only strengthened by the "racing" design, it is pared down to the bare minimum weight required.

"The wonderful thing," Svensson beams, "is that molded carbon fiber is a beautiful-looking material. So it's beautiful in its simplicity and its pure performance. We benefitted from the material usage."

As well, the team benefitted immensely from their close working relationship with Multimatic.

"From start to finish, Multimatic were fully integrated, part of the team," he says. "They brought an expertise in materials that we needed; they brought an expertise in suspension systems, in racing knowledge, so they were critical, as important as the designers or the Ford Performance engineers who were working on the car."

"The GT was 100 percent Ford conceived and designed from the perspective of what proportionally the car was going to be," Holt explains. "And then we packaged it: engine, gearbox, this, this and this and then we did all the aerodynamic work.

"A more cooperative relationship between engineering and design, I've never seen. And I may never see it again. The Ford guys are car guys. And if I said, 'No way that's going to work; it's going to be draggy or this or that,' they would change it! They…just…changed it."

Meanwhile, just a minor detail but, ultimately, Ford was proposing to compete in the 24 Hours of Le Mans in June of 2016 with a GTE-Pro class Ford GT whose first production counterpart was not targeted for delivery to its proud new owner until some six months after the race.

Although the FIA/ACO rules stipulate the timing and target numbers of production cars that manufacturers should achieve in order to go racing (an average of one car per week and a total of 100), the regulations also say in the event that a manufacturer isn't going to meet those targets, if the FIA and ACO consider it to be a serious production road car then they have the discretion to make the car "race" eligible.

"The timing of the car and our wish to race in 2016 when we were only going into production at the end of 2016, was made clear two years ago or longer," said Howard-Chappell. "The wording of the regulation around that was discussed in the Technical Working Group in which Mike Norton (Motorsport Manager, Ford of Europe) and I participate as Ford representatives, and the FIA and the ACO said that that should be possible."

Similarly, Howard-Chappell provided critical input through his understanding of the nuances of the WEC's 2016 rules package for the GTE-Pro class; rules that allowed for a more aggressive aerodynamic package than had previously been the case.

"I think I helped there," he modestly allows. "Along with Mike (Norton), I was the Ford representative when the rules were re-written to establish the latest GTE regulations. Therefore I was involved in the detail of drafting the new regs and understood not just the written text but the interpretation, i.e., what was intended."

In particular, the devices managing the airflow beneath the GTE-Pro cars (known as the front splitter and rear diffuser) had previously been permitted to extend no further back than the middle of the front axle (in the case of the splitter) and no further forward than the middle of the rear axle (in the case of the diffuser). The 2016 regulations allowed both devices to extend beyond the respective axles. These rules tended to favor mid-engined cars as the front-engine BMW M6, Corvette C7.R and Aston Martin Vantage were hard-pressed to take maximum advantage of the new front splitters; similarly the rear-engine Porsche 911 RSR only had so much room for the new rear diffusers.

"We understand the rules of the FIA, and we designed the car to meet those rules," says Svensson. "That's one of the benefits of understanding from the outset that you're going to go racing: you know the rules and regulations for that level or class of racing, and you design a car specifically to meet that criteria."

Indeed, one of the most noteworthy characteristics of the underside of both the road and racing versions of the Ford GT is that—just as a boat's keel directs the flow of water—the chassis incorporates a "keel" carefully shaped to direct a portion of the airflow to the splitter while "evacuating" the remainder of the airflow to the side exits in the bodywork. Not only does this enhance the performance of both the racing and road-going Ford GTs, it helps ensure the Ford GT race car meets the homologation standards requiring a high degree of similarity to its road car counterpart.

Notwithstanding Svensson's comments about designing the "car specifically to meet" the racing criteria, Holt and Howard-Chappell maintain that deciding whether the needs of the production car or race car took precedence in designing the Ford GT is akin to saying whether the chicken or the egg came first...

"I think it's a risk to read too much into the consideration of racing shaping the Ford GT design," says Howard-Chappell. "It was a clear objective from the concept phase that this car should be a groundbreaking road car in its own right. Therefore a lot of the time we were making sure that the road car features did not contravene any of the regulations for turning a road car into a race car, just as much as looking at what we might include to make a better racing car."

"The development was in parallel," says Holt. "Some people say 'You've compromised the road car in the service of making the race car fast.' But the road car is a performance car. Sure, if you want to go to the drive-in movie it's going to be a bit tight, but that's not what it's for. I would say that the high-performance road car has significantly benefitted from its race car pedigree: it's going to be a better, a lighter, a more efficient, more powerful, better handling, aerodynamically superior car than its competitors because it has so much to do with the race car."

Throughout the design process there was a constant dialogue among all of the parties, with the Toronto-based Holt spending two or three days at a time in Dearborn and attending the group's weekly meetings with Nair and Scott Keefer (Howard-Chappell's counterpart as project manager of the road version of the Ford GT); weekly meetings held on Wednesdays from 7 p.m. to 10 or 11 p.m.—sometimes later—in the name of secrecy and to enable everyone to focus on their "day jobs" at Ford.

The group in Dearborn supplied CAD files on the various components to Marcus and his colleagues at the Auto Research Center wind tunnel in Indianapolis, along with Multimatic's aero leader (and ex-Formula One/Indy car aerodynamicist) Dr. Mark Handford. In the early stages of the process, the aerodynamicists conducted CFD analysis on the components in order to, among other things, finalize the wheelbase and track width to maximize airflow efficiency.

They also evaluated the various styling themes from an aerodynamic standpoint, narrowing them to a couple of options from which the senior Ford management team—including Nair, Pericak and Motorsports Engineering Manager Mark Rushbrook—ultimately selected a single theme to take forward.

"The theme that was originally selected had some shortcomings," explains Marcus. "The front end was a little too bulky and had to be slimmed down. Also, the intercoolers were initially mounted in the nose of the car, and we pretty quickly realized that the original front end wasn't feeding them air very well. So we repositioned the intercoolers to the sides of the car, which worked out well. Initially, with the intercoolers up front, it was a packaging nightmare with those long lines running back to the engine, so it worked from both an aerodynamic and a packaging standpoint."

Not that the aerodynamic work ended with the repositioning of the intercoolers…or anything else.

"Everything we did had to be wind tunnel-tested," Svensson says. "It wasn't like a normal car program where you have a set time in the program where you are doing aerodynamic work with certain milestones in mind. This was just ongoing constantly; it never stopped."

Nevertheless, by the time Ganassi and Hull finally paid a visit to Dearborn, enough of the Ford GT had been finalized to get their attention in a big way.

"When you first saw the car it just took your breath away," says Ganassi. "It was obviously the grandson of the original Ford GT40 that had the hover board and the virtual reality headset on…but it still had the unmistakable family resemblance to the grandfather."

When the Ford GT "concept car" was unveiled at the 2015 North American Automobile Show in Detroit, the reaction was

Bill Ford, Mark Fields, Joe Hinrichs and Raj Nair

Giuseppe Risi

equally rapturous.

"It's an unmistakable shot across the bows of the world's preeminent supercar makers," said *Car and Driver*'s Alexander Stoklosa.

"The Ford GT was the most exciting, most innovative and most surprising meant-for-production car to make an appearance in 2015, period," wrote Robert Cumberford in naming the car *Automobile* magazine's Design of the Year in an article entitled *Ford GT: A Monument of Style, Inside and Out.*

Calling the Ford GT "a perfect example of function complementing design," *Top Gear*'s Jack Rix said, "assuming the GT performs like Ford claims, engineering perfection has never looked so good."

The Ford GT even became the first automobile to win a Gold Clio in the prestigious international Clio Awards competition.

When, after several months of speculation following the North American Automobile Show, Ford confirmed its plans to race the new Ford GT, the reception was even more enthusiastic in the motorsports community—particularly from some of those who would be competing against the Ford GT from Daytona to Le Mans.

"We heard from Porsche and Chevy that they were really glad Ford is back in the game," said Pericak. "Then in the next breath they said 'But did you have to bring a gun to knife fight?'"

"I was tremendously excited when Ford came back because Ford has a tremendous lineage in sports cars," said Giuseppe Risi, whose Risi Competizione is the most successful Ferrari GT racing team in North America, numbering three class wins each at Le Mans and Sebring among its achievements. "When many people think of Ford they think Ford makes trucks and sedans, but Ford's racing lineage is really incredible and not just in sports cars, but in Formula One, Indy cars, rallying and, of course, NASCAR. And then to have somebody like Chip Ganassi fly the flag for them, with his ability, with the results he's had in racing, I honestly don't think they could have chosen a better partner."

"I think if you went to BMW, Porsche and Ferrari, and certainly if you come to us, I'd say we all ought to be pretty flattered by the fact that Ford is showing up with a new Ford GT," said Fehan. "That name is revered. It's iconic, and for all of us, not just Corvette, it should be a proud moment that they're coming and I don't think that there's a manufacturer that doesn't look forward to competing with them. Because, although we may be enemies on the race track, when that checkered flag drops we're all in the same boat and we each have an oar and we've all got to paddle this thing forward."

But perhaps the most "on point" assessment was made by a journalist who, upon seeing the Ford GT at its unveiling at the North American Automobile Show, asked Pericak: "What did Ferrari do to piss off Ford this time?"

But was the beauty more than skin deep?

Chapter 3
Growing Pains

FOR ALL THE EXCITEMENT, emotion and even glamor associated with auto racing, when it comes to hard and often tedious work, few professional sports endeavors can match developing and testing a new race car. Anyone who has ever been within ten miles of a race track is familiar with the maxim *to finish first, first you must finish.* And while that chestnut applies to every form of motorsports—even races lasting less than four seconds and covering a quarter mile—it has a special relevance to sports car racing and its premier events which last six, 12 and 24 hours and often include the word "endurance" in their titles, official or otherwise. Forget speed: The first days, weeks and months of a new sports car's life are focused on reliability.

But before you can begin a development and testing program, you need a car. And, in the case of the Ford GT, the Multimatic test team needed one fast. After all when the Ford GT show car debuted in Detroit, the 2016 24 Hours of Le Mans was less than 18 months away…and the 2016 Rolex 24 at Daytona was just 54 weeks distant. What's more, there was still much work to be done by the designers, aerodynamicists and "packagers" before the specs were finalized for the prototype Multimatic would test and develop before building a second test car for the FCGR IMSA team.

"Time was ticking," said Charlie "Sandy" Cadieux, Multimatic's Manager of Vehicle Integration and Development, "and we really didn't know much about the car and what we were doing. Then it's: 'We have to have something ready in May,' and it was: 'WOW! I guess we better get going!'"

Charlie Cadieux

A small group at the Multimatic Technical Centre in Toronto including chief engineer Julian Sole and chief mechanics Neil Brodie and Mike Fletcher joined Cadieux in building the test race car essentially from scratch, initially engineering by PowerPoint to develop a battle plan before many of the basic materials and components were available.

"We didn't have a bill of material," Cadieux says. "It's not like you could order all these bits because a lot of them were still being invented and designed."

The most elemental building block was the Ford GT's carbon fiber tub, which was constructed at the Multimatic Technical Centre in the UK and shipped to Toronto. But what should have been the first big step in the process involved a small detour.

"The roll cage was a bit of a challenge," Cadieux says. "It was made out of 15CDV6 chrome moly tubing and, typically, here we make things out of 4130. So we had to bring in a guy who was familiar with 15CDV6 to weld it together—not because our guys couldn't, but because it was not what we were used to. Then it had to be bonded and bolted into the tub. It's not like we had many opportunities to re-do it: Once it was in it was in."

Meanwhile the group made preparations to assemble its high tech jigsaw puzzle.

"We started making cardboard boxes and locating things, making wiring looms out of tubes and plastic conduit, for an initial mock-up," Cadieux says. "I remember late one Sunday night trying to make a fuel cell out of a cardboard DHL shipping box—I'm sure it was a test to see how smart I am!"

Once the roll cage had been welded into the tub and painted, the group could start adding the actual bits and pieces as they became available...engine, gearbox, intercoolers, wiring, plumbing...bearing in mind the adage: How do you eat an elephant? One bite at a time.

"We build the tub and think: 'OK we've got a tub, we've got an engine and we've plumbed it...we've got a car now!'" he says. "Then all of a sudden it's: 'Yeah, hang a body on it.' That was another beginning. The nights were long and many.

"We had to do a makeshift body to hang on it, and it was like this body is not going to be the body, it was just the first set of bodywork. And then you makeshift it on and the Ford guys come and they stay up all night taping it and figuring where the (graphic) lines were going to be because the first car was going to be painted, even when we tested. So we shook-down with a car somewhat masked and primered, but just that whole process of getting the body fitted and getting them to agree on it was huge."

Against daunting odds the test car was ready for its initial shakedown run at Calabogie Motorsports Park near Ottawa on May 16 in Maxwell's hands, overseen by Holt, Howard-Chappell, Sole, Brodie, Fletcher, Sean Mason (Multimatic's Motorsports Manager) and Peter Gibbons (Multimatic's Technical Director of Vehicle Dynamics).

On the first day of a shakedown test it's not unusual for a car to spend more time in the pits than on the track. Job One is confirming the car's systems and mechanical components are working well and in relative harmony.

After the car has been fueled, the engine run to check for leaks, the Nomex-suited driver dons gloves, helmet and HANS device, slides into the seat and hooks-up his drink bottle and radio connections while a mechanic cinches his six-point safety harness. On a signal from the crew chief, the driver starts the engine, engages first gear, lets out the clutch and judiciously

Shakedown at Calabogie

pulls out of the pit stall, idles down the pit lane and takes to the track…slowly.

Assuming nothing catastrophic occurs like a fire caused by a leaky fuel system or an electrical short circuit, the driver invariably returns to the pits after one slow circuit of the track known as an "installation lap." The instant the car comes to a stop, mechanics swarm around checking for fluid leaks, loose parts, detached body panels, leaking tires or any of a myriad of things that could have gone wrong the first time such a fiendishly complex collection of parts and systems worked together at the same time on a race track, even at speeds most cars regularly exceed on the nearest highway.

Obviously, some issues are more significant than others. For example, a loose body panel, balky gear shifter, electrical problem or leaky fuel cell require immediate attention and, if not quickly fixable, halt the test until the problem can be properly addressed. On the other hand, if a driver can't see his rear view mirrors properly—and if there are no other cars sharing the track—the fix is added to the "to do" list and the test continues.

Once any issues have been attended to—and assuming none are test-stoppers—the driver gets the signal to refire the engine and return to the track.

Now it's time to begin to feel-out the car; for the driver to get a first inkling of how it performs in its current state; to begin developing a sense of its potential…and how to achieve it. With each lap the driver gets on the power a little harder, brakes a little later and turns into corners with increasing enthusiasm.

For most professional race drivers, it only takes half a dozen laps—at most—to develop a sense they are approaching the limits of the car's performance, or at least an idea of where those limits lie. A professional driver will also have begun assessing the car's strengths and weaknesses, and formulating his thoughts on what is needed to improve its performance.

In the case of the Ford GT's first laps at Calabogie, Maxwell found a lot to like.

"The first shakedown, you could tell right away it was a good car" he says, "and I've shaken-down some cars you couldn't say that! It felt right. I'm not saying there weren't issues: The brakes were not great, but it had gobs of downforce. That was my first comment—it had lots of downforce—and you could tell it was going to be a good car. How good I didn't know. I couldn't say: 'This is going to win Le Mans!' But I knew it wasn't a dog."

So too did Sole.

"The car ran very well out of the box from Day One," he said. "We had very few running issues; we were able to go to the track and, straight away, turn it on, start it up…it went 'round the track and it changed gears. It was all very, very positive, which was good because the early testing was all about getting miles on the car, getting the durability up. So actually being able to go out and put miles on it was a real bonus."

Under the direction of Holt, Howard-Chappell, Mason, Sole and Gibbons—and with O'Gara and Hennek often on hand to observe and lend a helping hand when needed—the development program continued through the summer…apart from a couple of interruptions when the one and only Ford GT race car was shipped to France in June for Ford's public announcement of its intent to compete in the 2016 24 Hours of Le Mans and, later, to the Michelin test track for evaluation by the FIA.

Until that point, the testing had been conducted at Calabogie. But Multimatic paid a visit to Canadian Tire Motorsport Park near Toronto in July on the Monday after the IMSA race there to gauge the Ford GT's speed in relation to the current competition. Would it be on the pace? Five seconds slower? Ten seconds slower?

Despite difficulties with the gearbox calibration, Maxwell got to within a couple of seconds of the previous day's race pace in about a dozen laps. Those favorable comparisons were confirmed a few weeks later when they tested the Ford GT at Road America during the week just before the IMSA race.

"At the end of the day they put me on a good set of tires and I matched the previous year's pole," says Maxwell. "Then on the race weekend they went about a second under that. But again, the car was close. We said, 'We've got a good car here. It's just a case of refining it.'"

By this stage, Johnson had joined the testing program and, together with Maxwell, the Multimatic duo had run the Ford GT for several thousand miles. Not only had it shown promising speed, according to Maxwell, it continued to be remarkably trouble-free.

"As spring turned into summer, Billy joined-in and we started putting in long runs, the car got better and better and better...and crazily reliable. I can't remember a day where we had to shut down early because of a problem."

As the testing program continued, Multimatic was hard at work building a second development car for Ford Chip Ganassi Racing's Indianapolis-based team to begin its own testing program. Having learned by doing constructing the first test car, they were able to build the second test car for FCGR in relatively short order. Following a successful shakedown test at Calabogie,

Julian Sole and Billy Johnson

the car was delivered to the Ganassi shop in Indianapolis on September 30 where, with the IMSA team already at Road Atlanta for the season finale, the Indy car mechanics installed voice and telemetry radios, harnesses and antennae, did a "nut 'n bolt" check and added discrete Ford Chip Ganassi Racing logos to its doors. Then they loaded their Ford GT on a nondescript "stealth" trailer and headed south where they would deliver the car to the IMSA team during the 18th annual Petit Le Mans.

There, with fans and competitors focused on the race, the Ford GT was to be unloaded in semi-secrecy and tucked under the Ford Chip Ganassi Racing tent away from prying eyes. Then, after the race, the EcoBoost Ford GT would be loaded on the transporter and taken to Daytona for a shakedown test of its own, while the EcoBoost Daytona Prototype that competed in Petit Le Mans was deposited in the unmarked trailer for transport back to Indianapolis.

At least that was the plan. But when a pounding rain forced officials to stop the race just past half distance, fans and competitors alike swarmed into the paddock...just as the mechanics rolled the Ford GT out of the unmarked trailer. With its unpainted gray-black carbon fiber bodywork, the car looked like nothing so much as the Ford GT Bruce Wayne might have on order. And as dozens of fans' cell phone camera flashes lit the Georgia gloom with a strobe-like effect, the mechanics wasted no time getting the car under wraps—and securing the transporter tent flaps.

As the drivers, O'Gara and several mechanics celebrated their second-place finish on the podium, Ganassi and Hull joined Pericak and Rushbrook giving the Ford GT the once over in the confines of the transporter tent. Later, after it had been wheeled back to the paddock, the confetti-covered EcoBoost DP sat virtually unattended in a corner of the tent as the mechanics and engineers pored over the Ford GT, getting their first up-close look at their future.

A few days later, the IMSA team joined the Multimatic squad at Daytona International Speedway for the first of four joint tests scheduled for October and November at Daytona (twice), Sebring International Raceway and Miami-Homestead Speedway.

Were this a Hollywood script, Day One of the first test at Daytona would have dawned with one of the Ganassi drivers sitting in the Ford GT, anxiously revving the engine, eager to

Shakedown at Daytona

scream out of the pits the instant the fellow holding the green flag in the starter's stand flinched.

In reality, most of the day was devoted to putting finishing touches on the car. No matter that Multimatic had incorporated "fixes" to the initial teething issues in their test car into the Ganassi mule. Whether it's a one-make, spec-chassis series with dozens of theoretically identical cars, or Formula One or sports prototypes where only a handful of cars are made, every race car is unique. Thus while the Multimatic Ford GT circulated the Daytona road course in the hands of Maxwell and Johnson, the Ganassi crew spent much of the day getting the rear floor panel on their Ford GT to fit exactly right. As the garage echoed to the sounds of hammers, grinding wheels and, on a radio tuned to a classic rock station, the Doobie Brothers, Fleetwood Mac and The Police, Hand and Pruett alternately paced and stood around like expectant fathers in a maternity ward. After a couple of hours of work, the rear floor pan finally slid into place…but in making it fit, two or three other panels that fit earlier had been moved slightly out of kilter.

This is precisely why teams test race cars: To learn how to extract a car's maximum performance to be sure, but also to learn which parts that look indestructible on CAD are, in fact, fragile; and to see which parts that fit together snugly on the prototype are misaligned, even slightly, on subsequent models. Make no mistake, however, when the Ford GTs made their race debut in late January, in the event of minor rear end damage during the Rolex 24 Hours of Daytona, instead of the six hours it took in the first test, installing a new rear floor panel would be the work of a minute—or less.

Did we mention that the right side door didn't latch properly? Or that electronics engineer Ken "The Silver Fox" Brooks scurried back and forth between the garage and the transporter's engineering office, laptop computer in hand, synching the car's on-board telemetry with the Ganassi systems? After all, no modern race team turns a lap in testing unless the engineers can download and analyze gigabits of data from a car's on-board computers.

All the while, Goldberg and Hennek huddled with Sole and Gibbons discussing baseline chassis/aerodynamic setups and a general plan for beginning to tune the car to the drivers' liking.

Finally, just after 4 o'clock, O'Gara gave Hand the signal to climb aboard the Ford GT. He fired the V6 turbo and drove the car to the pits where the crew made one final pass to ensure the bodywork was firmly attached—and changed to a new set of Michelins just in case a stray bolt or carbon fiber shard punctured a tire on the brief journey from the garage. Henceforth, the original four tires were designated as the "tow set" and installed every time the car traversed the two or three hundred yards between the garage and the pit area.

Finally, Hand started the engine, engaged first gear, slowly motored down pit lane, and disappeared around its 180-degree

Ken Brooks

exit bend before joining the track. Two and a half minutes later, he returned to pit lane so the crew could check for leaks, loose bodywork or anything else amiss. Given the OK to go, he returned to the track and gradually picked up the pace.

After about a dozen flying laps, Hand pulled onto pit road and turned the Ford GT over to Pruett. Although there was no painfully slow installation lap this time, Pruett was prudent for a lap or two before gaining real speed. He too only did a handful of laps before the checkered flag waved at 6 p.m. sharp, bringing the day to an end with smiles all around.

Hand and Pruett both reported the front end to be very "positive," so much so that it overpowered the rear. In other words, the Ford GT was generating so much grip on the front end that the rear end was pivoting around it. In a word, it was "loose."

"The front and rear seem disconnected. The front is so positive that the rear can't catch up," Hand said. "I don't feel like I can charge the turn. If you do, the front end hooks up, the tail comes out and you're sliding the first part of the turn.

"You can't lean on the rear," said Pruett. "It feels like it's propped up."

Nor did the brakes inspire confidence. This came as no surprise. Since the first shakedown test at Calabogie, Maxwell, Johnson and Hand (after a brief run in the Multimatic car at Sebring) had reported the brakes lacked "feel." Indeed, the only incident of note during the Multimatic testing program was an "off" at Sebring that Maxwell attributed to a lack of stopping power.

Nevertheless, the day was pronounced a success.

"It was a good day," said O'Gara. "We got some running and the car didn't catch on fire! Especially for a turbocharged engine that's a plus."

"I've never seen a turbo that didn't catch on fire at some point," quipped Goldberg.

Still, as expected, basic teething issues did arise. The cockpit brake bias adjuster knob was mislabeled, for example, so when Hand and Pruett tried to add more rear brake bias they instead shifted even more braking force to the front. The right side door popped open as Hand went down the back straightway at 150+ mph, and in the first few laps the Ford GT managed to shed the glass from both its external rear view mirrors.

So that evening, fabricator Bob Terando paid a visit to

a nearby Auto Zone to buy a couple of off-the-shelf mirrors. In the morning he would construct sturdy mirror mounts that would not vibrate and shake the mirror glass loose on the steep Daytona banking. On a car where upwards of 400 hours of wind tunnel and more than 2000 CFD tests had been run to generate the precise combination of downforce and airflow to the engine intakes, the cobbled together mirrors and mounts were positively Stone Age. But they'd do while permanent fixes were developed in conjunction with upcoming wind tunnel tests...

Meanwhile, Goldberg and Hennek put their heads together with O'Gara to map out a game plan for the morrow.

"Tomorrow we'll begin playing with the rear Gurney flap, the ride height," said Hennek "With the Daytona Prototype it was generally a case of keep going lower on the ride height until you hit the ground. That doesn't appear to be the case with the Ford GT. We're not even in the window yet."

The work of a season had begun.

Chapter 4
A Team of Le Mans
Assassins

IF FORD'S SELECTION OF MULTIMATIC and Chip Ganassi Racing
as partners in the Ford GT program rated as "no-brainers,"
choosing the drivers to pilot the cars in the IMSA WeatherTech
SportsCar Championship, FIA World Endurance Championship
and 24 Hours of Le Mans was considerably more complicated.
Forgetting for the moment its long-standing association with
Multimatic, there were only a handful of automotive engineering
companies in the world capable of partnering with Ford in the
simultaneous design, development and production of a super-
high performance road car and a GT race car (Holt would argue
the precise number of viable candidates is one—but then he is
biased).

Likewise, while Ford was enjoying a successful relationship
with Ganassi Racing, apart from Roger Penske, there wasn't
any other race team owner on the North American scene to
compare with Chip Ganassi when it came to resources and a
track record, particularly in a sports car racing arena that has
come to epitomize the organization.

"Chip Ganassi Racing started as an open-wheel/single-seat
team and in some respects that remains our 'signature' program,"
says Hull. "But what the organization is really all about is
epitomized by the sports car team, where we value individuality
and creativity but mainly as it contributes to the team. Chip
Ganassi Racing is about people, about letting people express
their creativity and talent in a way that helps the team grow."

There were dozens of talented, experienced race drivers who warranted serious consideration—and who would have given a kidney to be part of Ford's return to Le Mans. Discussing the plethora of applicants, Hull offers a glimpse into how and why Ganassi Racing has developed such a competent, dedicated and—yes—harmonious team of individuals.

"My phone was ringing off the hook with calls from drivers who wanted to be part of the program…understandably," he says. "I tried to listen to all of them, to treat them all with the respect they deserve. There's a lot of very good race drivers out there, some are best-suited to this team and this program, but they're all deserving of respect.

"That's not just some altruistic platitude," he continues. "I can learn something from every driver I speak with; and also, I can maybe help them and help us down the road. A driver—or for that matter a mechanic or an engineer—may not be the right fit for our team for any number of reasons. But I hear things and sometimes I can give a colleague a call and say, 'I hear you're looking for someone. I think so and so might be a good fit for

Mike Hull

your program. He didn't work out for us for such and such a reason, but I think he might work for you.'"

Ford Performance took a rather more analytical approach, developing an eye-straining spread sheet on the potential drivers. Based largely on drivers' Le Mans experience, the effort winnowed the list to a select group termed "Le Mans Assassins."

Although "assassins" was a bit over the top, perhaps self-consciously so, the idea was to assemble an elite list of drivers with current Le Mans experience who had proven they could do the job. Thus were created spread sheets showing a given driver's lap times at Le Mans in the day and night, dawn and dusk, rain, dry and damp, in practice, qualifying and race conditions in comparison to their co-drivers and teammates.

"We certainly wanted to have people with experience at Le Mans," says Nair. "We were willing to take maybe one or two rookies but, at Le Mans, if you have a rookie then you have to give up some track time for what amounts to rookie orientation.

"Chip is great at identifying and grooming young talent and in the past he used the DP program for that; but the GT program wasn't the program for that. It was for guys who are established, who are in their prime, and who can work together as a team. These are by definition team guys, whether it's guys who have worked together before or, as we went through the interview process, guys we could see are going to gel."

At least one choice amounted to a slam dunk. Not only had Joey Hand distinguished himself driving the Ford EcoBoost (and BMW-powered) Daytona Prototypes for Ganassi, he had raced at Le Mans in 2011, finishing third in a GTE-Pro class BMW M3 with Andy Priaulx and Dirk Müller.

Not surprisingly, the partners quickly added Müller to the lineup. In addition to sharing the third place BMW with Hand and Priaulx at Le Mans, Müller had a runner-up and a sixth-place finish at la Sarthe on his resume. What's more, Müller and Hand co-drove for Rahal Letterman Racing when they won the 2011 IMSA GT drivers championship following wins at Sebring, Long Beach and Lime Rock.

In some respects, a German version of the California-born and raised Hand, Müller's cheerful demeanor and impish looks belie the fact that he would turn 40 before the Ford GT ran its first lap in competition at the Rolex 24 Hours of Daytona. A family man in more ways than one, like Hand he carries the name of his daughter (Mina) on his helmet and planned to commute from

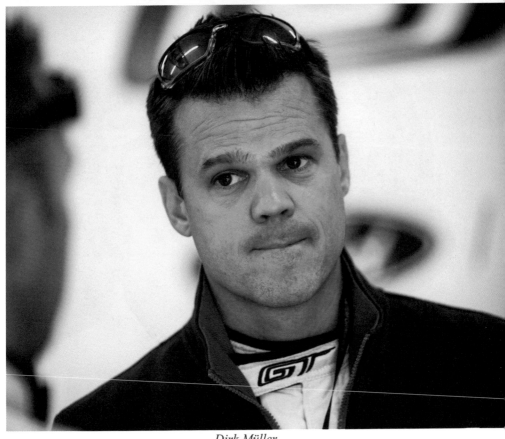

Dirk Müller

his home in Switzerland to his new "home" in the USA for tests and IMSA races.

"I'm still learning all the names from Ford and Chip Ganassi Racing, and at the same time I'm already home," he said. "It means a lot to my comfort level to be driving with Joey. It's a new program and a new team for me, but being with Joey again is like reuniting with family."

Speaking of reunions, it came as no shock when the team added Ryan Briscoe to the lineup. After all, the Australian had spent two separate stints driving Indy cars for Ganassi, first in 2005 and again from 2013-14. But that's just the tip of the iceberg on a resume that includes a stint as a test driver for Toyota's Formula One team and wins in IMSA and IndyCar. And not with just any teams. In addition to Ganassi, Briscoe drove for Penske, Wayne Taylor and Corvette Racing, the latter of which included an all too brief appearance at Le Mans in 2015 that ended when a stuck throttle during a practice session propelled co-driver Jan Magnussen into a guardrail, damaging the Corvette (but fortunately not Magnussen) beyond repair.

Ryan Briscoe

In a manner of speaking, the 2015 24 Hours of Le Mans reflected Briscoe's career. For, despite a slew of wins in Indy cars, sports and touring cars—not to mention pole position for the Indy 500—Briscoe was still looking for that signature victory to solidify his rightful position among the elite race drivers of his era.

A few days before the public announcement of the IMSA lineup, Briscoe flew to Indianapolis from his home in Connecticut to meet with the team at Chip Ganassi Racing's 80,000 square-foot race shop on 7777 Woodland Drive.

Briscoe takes it from there…

"I didn't want to be late for the meeting, so I got there plenty early—so early that I had time to go to the Starbucks down the road for a coffee. No sooner did I place my order than Joey (Hand) walked in…followed a few minutes later by Dirk (Müller) and we all had a good laugh. If a reporter had stopped for a coffee they'd have had the story on the Ford GT driver lineup a few days ahead of schedule."

At least three-fourths of the story. Richard Westbrook, the

Richard Westbrook

fourth member of the driving team, may have missed the memo on the pre-meeting gathering at Starbucks, but he fit with his new colleagues like coffee and biscotti…or breakfast tea with toast and marmalade. Something of a racing *tromp de l'oeil* in that he appears taller than his 5′11″ frame, the Englishman won back-to-back Porsche Supercups and raced as a Porsche factory driver before joining Corvette Racing, winning the 12 Hours of Sebring in 2013 and finishing fourth at Le Mans last year.

Whether owing to his natural reserve, the fact he was (by a few months) the greybeard of the four, or perhaps because a financially enforced sabbatical from racing in his twenties gave him a keen appreciation of his ultimate success, Westbrook seemed destined to play the role of the quartet's elder statesman. Not that his teammates were any less professional, committed or driven, but Westbrook carried about him a certain *gravitas* that contrasted to Briscoe's sunny countenance and the GenX demeanor of Hand and Müller.

Although the official announcement of the WEC team was months away, the fact that Marino Franchitti became a regular presence in the Multimatic team as the fall testing program progressed strongly suggested he figured in the plans for the coming season. Not so unlike Briscoe, Franchitti was looking to make his mark, a signature achievement if you will, that would enable him to move him out of the shadow of his older brother, Dario, a three-time Indy 500 winner, four-time IndyCar champion and Daytona 24 Hours winner—this despite the fact that Marino owned an overall win in the 12 Hours of Sebring in the FCGR EcoBoost Daytona Prototype as well as an LMP2 class win there (with Briscoe), to go along with a GTO title in the British GT Championship.

Like his sibling, Marino has an abiding interest in motorsports history and was keenly aware of both the possibilities—and the responsibilities—of racing the Ford GT at Le Mans.

"I love reading about the history of the sport, so I understand that the original Ford GT40 and the Ford Le Mans effort in the 1960s was a big deal," he said. "So to go back to Le Mans with a modern Ford GT is a big deal. Following in the footsteps of guys like Chris Amon, Bruce McLaren, (1967 winners) Dan Gurney, A.J. Foyt, (1968 winners) Pedro Rodriguez, Lucien Bianchi, (1969 winners) Jacky Ickx, Jackie Oliver...you're walking in the footsteps of giants."

Johnson too, seemed to be cementing his case for inclusion in the team in some capacity.

"Nobody has told me anything for sure," he said. "But they keep asking me to come to the tests...so that can't be a bad thing!"

By the same token, Olivier Pla's name could be added to the mix if his unannounced appearance at a Daytona test later in the fall meant anything...and "things" like that usually do. The Frenchman's career had hit a *cul de sac* of sorts when he signed with Nissan's short-lived LMP1 program in 2015, but the fact that the LMP2 class runner-up both at Le Mans and in the overall WEC standings in 2014 was regularly tapped as the third driver for long-distance events by the likes of Krohn and Michael Shank Racing testified to his stature in sports car racing circles.

Equally, his reaction to driving the Ford GT left little doubt that he wanted to be part of the program going forward.

"Most of my sports car racing experience is prototypes not GT cars, so I wasn't sure what to expect from the Ford GT," said the fiery-haired Frenchman. "By the second lap I had a big smile

Olivier Pla

on my face."

Scott Dixon was another likely candidate to spend time at the wheel of a Ford GT,—given the immense respect he commands within Ganassi Racing as the winningest active IndyCar driver, defending series champion and a regular "guest" driver for Ganassi's sports car program at the Rolex 24 at Daytona, 12 Hours of Sebring and Petit Le Mans. The fact that he too was conspicuous by his presence at a couple of Ford GT tests only fueled the suspicion he would be part of the program despite the fact that, never having turned a lap at la Sarthe, he hardly qualified as a "Le Mans Assassin." Then too, there were potential conflicts between Dixon's "day job" piloting Ganassi's Target IndyCar and the pre-race Le Mans schedule.

If tea-leaf readers could assume with some degree of confidence that Franchitti, Johnson, Pla and Dixon would be racing Ford GTs in 2016, however, the signs were less positive for Pruett and Maxwell. Following the IMSA team's initial tests at Daytona, Pruett was nowhere to be found two weeks later when the teams reassembled at Sebring.

Nor did the 55-year-old Pruett's name appear on the Le Mans Assassins list. While Ford and Ganassi offered him a veritable golden parachute in the form of a ride in the FCGR

Scott Pruett

EcoBoost Daytona Prototype at the 2016 Rolex 24 at Daytona and an open-ended role as an ambassador for Ford Performance, Pruett opted to drive the Action Express Daytona Prototype at Daytona prior to assuming a prominent role in the development of Lexus' new GT3 program.

"It's the end of our professional relationship, but not our personal relationship," Pruett told racer.com's Marshall Pruett of his parting of the ways with Ganassi. "It's been an incredible 12-year run, I couldn't be more appreciative and excited, and through no fault of Chip or mine, different opportunities were presented to the both of us and we had to follow what we thought was the best for us."

While Maxwell shared the driving duties on the Multimatic test car with Johnson and Franchitti at that Sebring test, he was growing increasingly resigned to the prospects that his services would not be needed when testing the Ford GTs turned to racing the Ford GTs.

"I've heard the rumblings," Maxwell said. "Face it, I'm 52 years old and from what I hear, there are some issues with age. I understand. I get it. I want to be part of it, but if I was Larry Holt or Chip Ganassi or Dave Pericak I'd be looking at young

Scott Maxwell

hot shoes too."

Maxwell had driven for Multimatic as both a race and a road car test driver since 1992. Thus he had been an integral part of the company's efforts to secure a manufacturer-supported effort to race at Le Mans for more than two decades, only to find that time had passed him by just as those dreams were realized.

"It's just that my timing is bad," he shrugged. "It is what it is, and I am lucky to have been part of it."

In contrast to Johnson, when he was invited to drive at subsequent tests, Maxwell politely declined.

"I said, 'If I'm not part of the race program, let's just leave it with the guys who are.'"

After only one full day (plus an hour or so the first day) worth of running at Daytona in October, the IMSA team planned to run a full 12 hours on the second of two days of testing at Sebring. Where better to "shakedown" a by now reasonably well-tested but still unproven car than at Sebring International Raceway, a 3.74-mile circuit built on a former World War II Army Air Force base featuring a mix of brutally rough and tumble runways and relatively smooth sections of macadam.

As the WEC car hammered around the track in the hands of Franchitti and Johnson, first Müller, then Westbrook and Briscoe slid into the IMSA test car for their first laps in a Ford GT. It didn't take long for them to understand what they'd gotten themselves into…

"Can you see the big smile on my face," beamed Müller after turning the car over to Westbrook. "That's a race car. Leaving the pits the first time I pushed the radio button and told the guys 'Thanks for letting me be part of this!'"

Later, over lunch, Briscoe observed, "When Richard came past the pits on his first lap I thought: 'Boy, he's going kind of fast.' But when I got in the car I saw why. You feel it's a race car from the moment you accelerate out of the pits."

Franchitti was not surprised.

"When I saw the Ganassi boys this morning I told them: 'This is the nicest new car I've ever driven.'"

Nice, but not perfect by any means. Although Hand was pleased with the progress in the car's handling—"at Daytona it was pretty evil, but now it's pretty good. We're confident we can get it in the window with basic changes"—the Ford GT's brakes continued to be confidence "un-inspiring." This despite a complete going over after the first test, including thoroughly cleaning the brake lines, rebuilding the calipers, and bringing a range of new brake pads to Sebring.

"The longer you run the less effective they become," said Hand, who took a turn in the car later in the day. "We bled them after the first couple of runs, but it hasn't changed anything."

The following day the foursome embarked on a 12-hour test at 10 a.m. Some eleven and half hours later they cut it ever so slightly short when Hand dropped a wheel off the track into a sizable chuckhole. Although the mechanics found no damage to the car, the team decided not to push their luck after what had been a startlingly trouble-free test. In just its third full day, the IMSA team's Ford GT had absorbed nearly 12 hours of Sebring-style punishment with just two minor problems. First, a crewman knocked a brake duct loose during a tire change late in the afternoon. Second, a couple of hours after the brake duct had been (quickly) reattached the gear shifts became erratic, necessitating a relatively brief stop to recalibrate the gear position sensors.

Period.

Chapter 5
Transitions

With the Ganassi test car now running in tandem with the Multimatic Ford GT, Howard-Chappell's "transition" from project director of the Ford GT race car to team manager for the FCGR WEC race team accelerated. With some key personnel already in place from the Multimatic test program, Howard-Chappell began scouting locations for the team's UK base, eventually deciding on a shop in Greatworth Park, Oxfordshire. The former home of British Touring Car Championship powerhouse Triple Eight Racing, it was little more than a shell of a building when Multimatic took possession of the facility in November.

Thus all that remained to be accomplished in the coming weeks was to continue the process of recruiting additional personnel and developing a cohesive team, build a state-of-the-art race shop in time for the public announcement of the WEC driver lineup in early January and, as the Multimatic facility in Toronto increasingly turned its focus to the production car, build two new Ford GT race cars in time for IMSA's Roar Before the 24 test on January 17-18...all the while beginning to create an inventory of spare parts and equipment.

"I got off the plane, met George at the shop and the first thing we did was go to the UK version of Home Depot to get paint and two rollers," recalls Cadieux. "Then we started painting the upper floor of the shop so we could come back (after the paint dried) and start uncrating the inventory that had been shipped from Canada so we could make a makeshift parts department upstairs. At the same time we were building race cars for

Daytona.

"You had to make something of nothing out of that facility, and it started to wear on you. We had nothing. We had to go next door to David Appleby, a very nice man who was looking after the facility. He could see what we were up against and we would be asking: 'Do you have a dash-three or a dash-four fitting because I really need to plumb this line and we've got nothing?' And the battle was just beginning at that point in time."

Although there was a Herculean amount of work to be done, the shop's location was a bonus in the recruitment of talented/ veteran personnel.

"As we were in what we call 'Motorsports Alley' in Oxfordshire the gene pool is extremely good," says Howard-Chappell. "So we were able to get a core of extremely knowledgeable, experienced guys together who knew how to go GT racing and how to build a car.

"As with most things it's down to the people...I won't say it was easy, but it was possible."

However, Holt and Howard-Chappell faced something of a delicate balance in completing the staffing of the race team. On the one hand, they wanted to include a meaningful number of Multimatic employees to emphasize the company's racing expertise; on the other hand, they didn't want to "gut" Multimatic's roster to the point that the other racing programs suffered. Nor did they want to mount an unseemly "raid" on Howard-Chappell's former employer (ProDrive).

Thus they targeted a roughly 50/50 mix between Multimatic staffers and new hires from the racing community at large. In addition to Sole, Fletcher and Brodie, young Multimatic vehicle dynamicist Vince Libertucci was added to the roster; as well, Russell Paddon (a protégé of Multimatic's Dave Williams who was instrumental in developing the Lotus F1 active suspension system) joined ProDrive veteran Dave "Wilks" Wilcock as one of the team's lead race engineers.

"We took a mixture of guys," says Howard-Chappell. "Some of the key people who we recruited early were people I knew from my past. A lot I had worked with before, some came from ProDrive AMR (Aston Martin Racing), because they were still working there; some had left about the same time I left and gone off to do something else. Then when they heard this program was getting going they were interested to know if I needed people—and for sure I did."

"Woody," "Wilks" and Howard-Chappell were reunited on the WEC team

In addition to Mark Paulin, chief mechanic on the test team, the veterans joining the program included sub-assembly chief John Ogden and team administrator Carol Melville.

"The minute that something was kicking off here I got in touch with Carol as she had always said anything I was involved in she wanted to hear about," Howard-Chappell says. "That was immediate—almost the first recruit."

The WEC team's veteran lineup also included Jonathan "Woody" Woodward, another refugee of Nissan's ill-fated LMP1 program and who had worked off and on with Howard-Chappell since their Lotus Formula One days. Some of their greatest shared success came campaigning Ford Mondeos in the 2000 British Touring Car Championship, a season when Ford won the manufacturers title, ProDrive the team title and Alain Menu, Anthony Reid and Rickard Rydell finished 1-2-3 in the drivers championship.

"We absolutely cleaned up," says Woodward. "So my last experience with Ford was very good.

"Henry Ford is my hero. That guy did more to change the

world than anybody, in my view. What an absolute genius; farmer's boy to one of the richest men in the world. Unbelievable. One of his sayings is: 'Whether you believe you can achieve something or you believe you can't—you're correct.'"

However, even the most powerful dose of positive thinking wasn't enough to meet the original goal of providing the IMSA team with two complete race cars (in addition to their test car) in time for the start of the 2016 season. Instead, Multimatic delivered a new tub to Indianapolis in early December with basics like plumbing and wiring looms installed, but which their colleagues then had to complete with parts cannibalized from the test car. A couple of weeks later a complete new car was delivered to Indianapolis via Toronto.

Not that any of it was as easy (or simple) as it sounds, on either side of the Atlantic.

"The first tub we had shipped on December 8 and felt bad we had to do that, but otherwise the other car would have never shipped by December 17th," says Cadieux. "We shipped the second complete car on December 15th to Toronto so that Sean (Mason) and the composite guys could hang the body on it and get it to the Ganassi guys for December 23rd.

"We had some mistakes in that car…There was a fitting that was put on the heat exchange and we plumbed it right up to the water header tank and—of course—it was oil. So basically we ran the car maybe ten minutes, just long enough that a little oil got in, but when they got it and ran it they had oil pumping into their cooling system. So the first thing they had to do after getting their new car was take the engine out: Merry Christmas.

"I'm sure it was awful for them; it was awful for us, but you make mistakes when you're up against it—and we were up against it. The days were long and many.

"You never knew what was around the corner; that what should have been a simple task became a monster job.

"We had these splined torsion bars that go through the rocker and into the keel. Today, it's a two-minute job; you just pop it in. I remember the first day getting the biggest hammer we had in the shop and just beating on it for 15 minutes. But that's what we had: one set of torsion bars and they had to go in—they might never come out, but they had to go in and they were going in that day. You look back now and you kind of laugh, but I can tell you that day I wasn't laughing…"

Humor was in equally short supply at 7777 Woodland Drive.

"I think I had one and a half days off in December," recalls Damon Elff, lead mechanic on the car driven by Hand and Müller. "The second car we got from Multimatic was supposed to be the easy one. The first thing we had to do was change the engine. We worked half a day Christmas Eve, took Christmas off and were back in the shop the next morning."

The pace was no less brutal at Greatworth Park where, miraculously, the shop was ready to host the public announcement of the second wave of Le Mans Assassins on January 5.

To those who'd been paying attention to the lineup at tests, it came as no surprise that Franchitti and Pla were front and center. Nor, in the final analysis, should it have come as a shock they were joined by two drivers with whom key members of the Ford GT program were quite familiar: Andy Priaulx and Stefan Mücke.

In addition to teaming with Hand and Müller in their run to third place at Le Mans with BMW, Priaulx had three World Touring Car Championships, a European Touring Car Championship and wins in the 24 Hours of the Nürburgring and 12 Hours of Sebring to his credit. Born and raised within

Marino Franchitti

Andy Priaulx

sight of France on the Isle of Guernsey (where he still resides), Priaulx exudes a professional but personable charm and—at age 41—an almost boyish enthusiasm that came through when he spoke about his decision to join the Ford GT program after 14 seasons with BMW.

"It is such a historic program," he said. "Every race driver wants to make history and every time you drive this car you make a bit of history. To be fully in a program like this at a high level, supported by a manufacturer like Ford, seeing the passion—they really want to win this. They really have been uncompromising and, for me, that's the environment I enjoy; that what it's all about. The passion is something that makes you want to get up in the morning and go do your job—and there's bags of passion here at Ford."

One would have to make an effort not to like the gregarious and refreshingly uncomplicated Mücke. Clearly Howard-Chappell was also fond of the performances he regularly delivered during their association with ProDrive Aston Martin Racing, including half a dozen WEC GTE-Pro class wins and a

Stefan Mücke

couple of podium finishes at Le Mans.

At age 34, the Berliner already had ten starts at Le Mans under his belt and was looking forward to number 11 with the same enthusiasm he felt, if not his first time there, every year afterward.

"When I am the first time at Le Mans I was, 'OK here we are, another endurance race only a little bit longer, but it's exactly the same as all the others,'" Mücke said. "But I tell you it's something completely different, what I learned ten years ago when I did my first Le Mans. It's an awesome feeling everything around it, the whole week of preparation for that one race. The spectators, everything...There are not really words for it. You need to live it, you need to feel it."

In subsequent weeks FCGR confirmed the names of several additional drivers who would be living and feeling the 24 Hours of Le Mans with the Ford GT program, including Bourdais (who would also be living and feeling the 12 Hours of Sebring and the 24 Hours of Daytona on the IMSA team) along with Harry Tincknell and Johnson on the WEC team.

What 24-year-old Tincknell may have lacked in experience he made up for with results. Mentored by no less than triple Le Mans winner and 2013 WEC champion Allan McNish, Tincknell enjoyed a promising single-seater career before switching to sports cars in 2014 and promptly winning the LMP2 honors in his Le Mans debut. Like Pla and Woodward, he joined Nissan's ill-fated LMP1 team for 2015 and was left high and dry when the Japanese automaker cut its losses after the season—but not before he set the fastest times in the Nissan GT-R LM Nismo at Le Mans in qualifying and the race itself.

Keenly aware of his position as the "junior" driver on the team, Tincknell intended to make the most of his opportunities—with FCGR as well as with co-drivers with Priaulx and Franchitti.

"It's a great situation for me because I'm the youngster coming in, but I have teammates to learn from with a lot of experience and I'm really feeding off that," he said, with a smile that would brighten Pridhamsleigh Cavern in his native Devonshire. "Since I was born they've been in car racing, winning and doing well, winning world championships, so it's absolutely invaluable for me to pick up on and take that into the

Harry Tincknell

rest of my career and make the most of it.

"I've always been striving to make on a team at this level. To actually be here and achieve it is fantastic...now that I'm here I have to stay here!"

For Johnson getting the nod to join the WEC team, to test and race on circuits he'd only seen on television like Silverstone, Spa, Monza, Paul Ricard and, of course, Le Mans was not only just deserts for the time and energy devoted to testing the Ford GT, but for his years developing, testing and racing a multitude of other Fords.

"From the development on the street car side of things and to have raced Mustangs for many years; and also to have opportunities to race in NASCAR...to be able to stay with Ford through all these things is just fantastic," he said. "Then to be involved with a program of this magnitude that is probably one of the most meaningful things in motorsports for Ford is just a huge honor.

"And, along with Joey, to be one of two Americans in the American brand is a big, big deal. I'm just happy to be here. Ford, Multimatic and Chip Ganassi have put together an awesome group of guys and I'm enjoying every minute of it.

Back in Indianapolis, the IMSA program was engaged in some team-building of its own. For all its success over the past dozen years, Ganassi's sports car program had been a one-car effort but for a single race each season (the Rolex 24 Hours of Daytona) when they fielded a second car maintained by members of the IndyCar team who, typically, did not run their first race until March. Testing, developing and racing two brand-new Ford GTs required both a reshuffling and a bolstering of the team's most important asset.

"Chip Ganassi Racing has always been about people; about accelerating people's growth within the system by taking on or expanding projects and programs," says Hull. "We have our own internal ladder system, so when we chose to do this project and move on to two full-season IMSA entries...the Darwinian process here is to find people on the shop floor, or in the engineering office, or in the job shops—wherever that might be—and give them opportunities to make an inter-company transfer as it were, to take on increased responsibility.

"Tyler Rees (chief mechanic on the Hand/Müller car) is an example: He was a rear end mechanic on Scott Dixon's Indy car for a long, long time, patiently awaiting the opportunity to become a chief mechanic. We gave him that opportunity."

In fact, Rees' apprenticeship dates to his days as a Boy Scout in a troop led by scoutmaster Grant Weaver, crew chief on Ganassi's 1996 IndyCar championship team and, for the past 18 years, shop manager of the team's Indianapolis facility. The father of four Eagle Scouts himself, Weaver helped guide Rees through the demanding Eagle Scout process—and found a future chief mechanic in the bargain.

"I grew-up wanting to be a service manager in a Chevy dealership," Rees explains. "Thanks to Grant, I spent a couple of years in high school as an apprentice in the race shop and, after I graduated, they offered me a job. On my first day Grant gave me a bucket of bearings and told me to clean them. When I finished, he took one look and said, 'They're not clean enough. Do it again.' They looked clean to me...but not to Grant."

Ashley Parlett is another example. A mechanic on Jamie McMurray's CGR NASCAR entry, she traded in the traveling grind of the 36-race Sprint Cup schedule for a position in Ganassi's Charlotte shop in order to free up weekends to work on the Ford GTs at IMSA races.

Goldberg traveled a much shorter distance to join the sports car team, moving across the Indianapolis shop from his post as race engineer on Charlie Kimball's Dallara Indy car. But make no mistake, were Ganassi Racing to expand into snowmobile racing and require his services, Goldberg would relocate to the North Pole. A few years back, when a family emergency cropped up in the middle of the season, Goldberg found round-trip plane tickets and a rental car had magically materialized—along with an open-ended leave of absence.

"I'll work for this team as long as they want me," he says. "I'd step in front of a bus for Chip."

Not every position is filled from within. Sometimes new blood is needed, indeed welcomed—so long as the blood types are compatible.

"We look for people who understand it takes equal participation to be successful," says Hull. "People who are very unselfish, who don't exude ego, have ears and eyes that actually work and have a communication style that engages everyone around them: those are the keys to success.

"What's nice is we have a corral full of people who have engaged each other like that for a long, long time so that anyone

Neal Goldberg and Richard Westbrook

coming in from the outside gets right up to speed. All those sheriffs create the posse that keeps everybody engaged."

Case in point, Brett Knostman. Crew chief on KVRT Racing's 2011 Indianapolis 500-winning car, he joined FCGR in early January after KVRT downsized for 2016.

"I worked in IndyCars with Kris Badger for years," Knostman says. "He had come over to Ganassi and was telling me all about the GT program and what a nice deal it is here… and also I'd talked with people here before.

"From the top to the bottom, whether it's the IndyCar side or the sports car side, everybody at Ganassi works toward the same goal from the engineers, to the machine shop, the painters, the carbon shop, the bodywork guys…everybody helps everybody out. It's amazing to come to a place with such a depth of skill, ability and resources. You can talk to the engineers or Grant (Weaver)—he's got a huge wealth of knowledge about stuff that I haven't seen before—and you'll get answers.

"The communication…if you have a problem you can go talk to the engineer, or if he has problems or wants you to do something different, everybody is moving forward all the time. If there's a problem you look back at it, figure out how to fix it so it never happens again and then you move on.

"Stuff just happens here. You ask for something in the afternoon and the next morning there's a new part ready to go into the car. Everybody knows their job, knows what they have to do and the quality of their work is incredible."

Whether a team member comes from the lower rungs of Ganassi Racing's internal ladder—or jumped on along the way—they find themselves in an environment focused on success. Now.

"I read something the other day that I think absolutely defines what we do at Chip Ganassi Racing," says Hull. "The Dalai Lama said, 'There are two days in your life that don't matter: yesterday and tomorrow.'

"When people move into a new role or new people come into our system, they're working with a group of people who are bound and determined to win today. They're gonna win on the shop floor, they're gonna win in the machine shop, they're gonna win in the engineering office and guess what? When they go to the race track they're gonna do the same thing.

"That's pretty hard to get people to do, but Chip lives and breathes that life; that's where it came from and that's how it's been built here. And once (people) have exhaled the first time, then it all starts to fall into place for them and—once you've nurtured them along—the sky's the limit."

Chapter 6
Shadow Play

CALL IT MANAGED COMPETITION, balanced performance or leveling the playing field, the desire of motorsports organizations to prevent a single team, car or manufacturer from dominating the competition is commonplace. After all, how many fans will pay their hard-earned money—or spend hours in front of their flat-screen TVs—watching a race where the outcome is virtually predetermined by the convergence of the laws of physics and R&D budgets. And what manufacturer is going to invest tens, perhaps hundreds, of millions of dollars competing in a series where a set of immutable rules consign its cars to finishing among the also rans?

One path taken by an increasing number of race sanctioning bodies is mandating that only a limited number (that number oft times being one) of different chassis and engines built to rigidly controlled specifications are eligible to compete in a given series. In theory, the resulting "spec" racing classes not only create even competition where the outcome is determined by driver skill and team performance rather than technology, they control the cost of racing since teams have no incentive to design and fabricate proprietary new parts, let alone entire chassis or engines.

On the other hand, from the day when primitive automobiles first raced along the dusty roads of Europe and North America, drivers, mechanics, teams and manufacturers have searched for any technical advantage to give themselves a leg-up on the competition. The racing cars that stir the souls and the imagination of fans and competitors alike are not the homogenized appliances of spec racing series, but innovative creations like the

D-Type Jaguar, Colin Chapman's Lotus Formula One cars and Jim Hall's Chaparral sports cars, the Porsche 917s and Ferrari 512s of the early 1970s, the Peugeot and Audi diesels of the 2000s and, of course, the Ford GT40. What's more, automotive manufacturers have long used racing as a testbed for developing new technologies—and giving employees experience exploiting those technologies in a highly pressurized environment.

Balance of Performance rules are sanctioning bodies' effort to have their technically innovative cake and eat it too; to enable a variety of different cars to compete in an environment where no competitor enjoys such a degree of technical superiority that—driver error, mechanical failures or acts of God apart—a race's outcome is a foregone conclusion before the cars roll off the transporters for practice and qualifying.

IMSA and FIA typically "balance" the performance of the cars by adjusting a few factors, specifically engine power, vehicle mass, fuel volume (tank size) and the refueling restrictor. Each adjustment has an effect on vehicle performance or pit stop time, both of which are critically important to winning races.

Engine power adjustments affect a vehicle's ability to accelerate and its top end speed which, in the final analysis, is governed by power versus aerodynamic drag. For naturally aspirated engines the adjustments are made through increasing or decreasing the volume of air passing through the engine's air restrictors and by limiting or increasing "boost" (manifold pressure) on turbocharged engines.

Vehicle mass adjustments affect almost all performance aspects of the car including its ability to accelerate but also its ability to decelerate (brake) and change direction (corner), and will also have an effect on tire and brake wear.

Adjustments to a car's fuel capacity and refueling rig restrictors are designed to ensure all cars in a given class can run approximately the same number of laps on a single tank of fuel, and that no car has an advantage or disadvantage based on the amount of time it takes to fill the fuel tank during a pit stop.

As can be imagined, however, balancing performance becomes extremely complicated when the rules permit a variety of very different automotive platforms to compete, as is the case in the GT classes of the IMSA WeatherTech SportsCar Championship and the FIA World Endurance Championship where front-engined Aston Martins, BMWs and Corvettes go head-to-head with mid-engined Ferraris and Ford GTs and rear-engined Porsches. Further complicating matters is the fact that the Aston Martin Vantage and Corvette C7.R are powered by normally aspirated 4.5- and 5.5-liter V8s, respectively, and the Porsche 911 RSR by a normally aspirated 4.0-liter, flat six. On the other hand, the BMW M6 GTLM features a turbocharged 4.4-liter V8 and the Ferrari 488 GTE a turbocharged 3.9-liter V8. The Ford GT? That would be the EcoBoost twin-turbo, 3.5-liter V6.

Suffice to say, developing a rules package to "balance" the performance of such a diverse collection of cars is not the work of a moment. Literally. IMSA and WEC Balance of Performance regulations are not cast in stone at some arbitrary date months in advance of the start of the season; rather they are announced prior to the season and then subject to regular review and adjustment based on information as basic as practice, qualifying and race lap times, and as complicated as wind tunnel testing and detailed analysis of the mountains of stupefyingly complex telemetry generated by modern racing cars.

And while they share data and (for the first time in 2016) collaborate in conducting joint tests of the cars in question,

BoP regulations for the EcoBoost V6 were informed by two years of experience.

Geoff Carter

IMSA and FIA independently set their own BoP.

In the case of the Ford GT, the fact that the 3.5-liter EcoBoost engine was something of a known quantity—having powered the Ford Daytona Prototypes for several seasons—gave IMSA a good starting point.

"We have some background on the car, on the engine and specifically the way they map the turbo boost," explains Geoff Carter, IMSA WeatherTech SportsCar Championship Senior Series and Technical Manager. "So that is our benchmark or baseline for understanding the performance on the new Ford GT; different class, different car but same power train."

In the fall of 2015, the manufacturers each shipped one of their cars to Michelin's test facility in Ladoux, France, where they underwent standardized tests under the watchful eyes of Carter's counterparts Dennis Chevrier (FIA Technical Delegate for the WEC) and Thierry Bouvet (ACO International Technical Delegate)—at least that was the plan. Inclement weather prevented officials from conducting a final set of tests on the Corvette C7.R and the Ford GT. As a result, IMSA's tests in the

Windshear Wind Tunnel facility in Charlotte, NC, in December would be used for the aerodynamic baselines on both cars, along with simulation work and dyno tests on one of each car's engines at the NASCAR R&D Center.

In simple terms, Carter and company had two sets of targets. The first was to ensure there would be a four percent differential between the two divisions of the prototype class (IMSA Daytona Prototype and LMPC/FIA LMP1 and LMP2) and the GT class (IMSA GTLM and GTD/FIA GTE-Pro and GTE-Am); second they aimed for a 0.3 percent differential (or 0.3 seconds in a 100-second lap) between the different makes of cars within a given class.

The tests at Ladoux and Charlotte, along with information supplied by the manufacturers, gave Carter and his FIA counterparts a baseline on which to begin developing the BoP regulations for the start of the season. Series-wide tests at Daytona in mid-December (known as the BoP Test) and mid-January (The Roar Before the 24) enabled IMSA to gather massive amounts of real world data on the prototypes and GTs expected to participate in the Rolex 24 and to fine-tune the BoP regulations for the start of the season.

Needless to say, the information is highly detailed...and proprietary.

"There's an understanding that the integrity of the data is super important," said Carter at the Roar Before the 24, "the protection of that integrity from the team side, and the validation of the integrity from the series' standpoint. And the magic word is 'transparency'—but the definition of transparency on either side is perhaps a little different!

"The idea is for IMSA to have as many marques as we can here for all the classes, to provide a platform with some different balance of performance changes; different weights, perhaps different restrictors and in the case of the turbocharged cars, specifically the BMW, Ford GT and Ferrari, different boost mapping.

"We take the logged vehicle data which we're requiring, run the cars through tech to validate their configuration. Then we've got a private file of all the timing and scoring data. We do our standard analysis and then we go back and validate or correlate this to our simulation and the information that came from the simulation data sheets the manufacturers provided to the FIA... and the manufacturers have to be pretty accurate there. Then we validate that."

All well and good, but the fact remains this is racing and teams are loathe to show their hand in testing lest the competition glean even the slightest bit of information—for example how much faster they need to go to match the pacesetters—that will enable them to come to the race (in this case, the Rolex 24 at Daytona) with an edge.

"Obviously, it's in the interest of teams and manufacturers not to display their full capabilities to their competitors and even the sanctioning body," says Howard-Chapell. "But the sanctioning body has to have access to data, so they can get a good idea of a car's capabilities. If you go too fast you risk getting an unfavorable BoP; if it's obvious that you're sandbagging (deliberately running short of a car's true capabilities) you risk getting your wrists slapped with worse performance hindrances than if you run too fast!"

The problem facing the IMSA technical group—and their FIA counterparts staging similar BoP tests (the WEC Prologue) at France's Circuit Paul Ricard in March—is sifting through the time sheets, sector times, throttle and brake traces and even GPS records of a car's positioning on the track to separate the wheat from the chaff; to identify who is and who isn't sandbagging; and by how much.

"If you want to take your stopwatch and spend your time timing your neighbor, that's on you," says Carter, "but we're not going to provide timing information beyond fastest laps in a given session. So the idea is that not everybody knows what everybody else is doing; go run your test plan and if you want to run at 80 percent, 82 percent, 92 percent to protect whatever—we understand that as a series."

Indeed, Carter reported that every one of the cars participating in the Daytona test showed some signs of "performance management," be it constantly running full fuel loads, short shifting, braking early, running the wrong gears to limit RPM or not using full or (in some cases) any throttle.

"In NASCAR Turn 4, coming onto the front straightaway there were cars where the driver had completely lifted and the throttle position was zero!" he grinned.

Keeping the competition in the dark is one thing but, as Howard-Chappell noted, woe betide the team or manufacturer who deliberately tries to mask its true performance from the officials. A team or manufacturer caught deliberately trying to mislead the sanctioning bodies faces penalties ranging from draconian BoP weight, power and aerodynamic "adjustments" to the FIA's dreaded "stop and hold" where a car is held in the pits for five or more minutes during the race, effectively eliminating any hope of victory.

In practice, the Balance of Performance is viewed by competitors as a necessary evil. At best.

"It's an imperfect solution," Howard-Chappell concedes. "But it does enable very different cars from a host of manufacturers to compete in as humanly as possible a fair and level playing field."

Still, no matter how hard the sanctioning bodies tried, no matter how sophisticated their data-capturing capabilities, no matter the class, the IMSA and WEC paddocks were usually rife with suspicion that one manufacturer or another was sandbagging.

"It's not about the best, fastest, most reliable car," commented one FCGR driver. "It's about who has the best, fastest, most reliable car…and can keep it under wraps until the right moment: then GO!

"So when does a car show its true potential? *Never*. If you do, you risk BoP corrections."

"Unfortunately, with Balance of Performance it limits the incentive to develop the greatest performance from your car," said Marcus. "Do a good job and you risk being penalized. Do a poor job and you stand a chance of being rewarded."

A look at the scoring monitors during the BoP and Roar Before the 24 tests did nothing to dissuade observers from concluding they we were witnessing a high-speed shadow theater, where actors standing behind a screen are back-lighted, so the audience sees their silhouettes on the screen rather than the actors themselves.

A typical practice session would begin with a couple of slow laps by each car, and then their speeds would increase incrementally—almost as if by magic improving in lock step with their competitors, a few tenths of a second each lap, seldom if ever going more than a tenth of a second or two faster that the "bogey" time of the fastest car in that class in that session… leaving observers to ponder whether the sanctioning bodies got the BoP exactly right; or whether the team with the quickest car in a given session did not want to show its hand to the other competitors…or the sanctioning body.

So when a Ferrari 488 (1:45.266) edged the Westbrook/

John Hennek

Briscoe/Mücke Ford GT (1: 45.269) for top honors by 0.003s in one Roar Before the 24 practice session—with the Hand/Müller/ Bourdais Ford GT, two BMWs and another Ferrari blanketed by 0.004s right behind—was it because the BoP regulations hit the proverbial nail on the head…or because, as Hennek colorfully explained "It's like being in a row of nails. You don't want to be the nail that's sticking up higher than the rest, or the sanctioning body will come along with a hammer and pound you down to the same level as the others."

Whatever the reality may or may not have been, based on the data collected at the BoP test and the Roar Before the 24, IMSA "adjusted" the performance of the Corvette C7.R, Ford GT and Ferrari 488 by reducing engine power at all engine speeds by roughly the same amount; the BoP adjustments to the BMW M6 increased power above 6500 rpm, but decreased power below that same threshold while the regulations for the Porsche 911 RSR remained unchanged.

Chapter 7
We Never Saw That Before!

ONLY A FEW MINUTES REMAIN in the 2016 Rolex 24 at Daytona and attention is fixed on an epic battle for the GTLM class victory. Barring last-minute mechanical failures or driver error, the Extreme Speed Motorsports Ligier-Honda has the overall win well in hand, while the PR1/Mathiasen Motorsports ORECA is miles clear of its closest competitor in the Prototype Challenge class. Yes, GTD honors still hang in the balance, but the Fox Sports cameras—and the multitudes of sleep-deprived fans lining the infield section of the road course—only have eyes for the (nearly) no holds-barred intra-Corvette Racing contest between the lead C7.R of Oliver Gavin and its clone, driven by Antonio Garcia.

Lap after lap Garcia swings this way and that in Gavin's wake as the 'Vettes cross the start/finish line and thunder into Turn One. Every time the Spaniard sniffs an opening, the Brit firmly but cleanly parries his thrust as both drivers flirt with the unthinkable: throwing away a certain 1-2 finish for Corvette Racing in pursuit of individual glory.

Meanwhile, unnoticed but for a few dozen eyeballs in the FCGR pits, mechanics swarm about the #67 Ford GT which has pulled onto pit lane. The transmission problems that have afflicted both Fords throughout the past 22 hours have struck again, leaving Westbrook stuck in neutral almost within sight of the finish. These and other mechanical problems have long since eliminated the EcoBoost Ford GTs from contention, and while the #66 continues circulating in seventh spot in class, the #67 is in ninth place a whopping 130 laps down on its sister car—and 127 laps in arrears of the #911 Porsche, albeit five laps clear of its nearest GTLM rival, the #77 Ferrari.

With five minutes remaining, Westbrook has no more chance of catching the Porsche for eighth place than the Ferrari has of overtaking his immobile Ford GT for ninth. Pride alone is at stake: Pride in the designers, engineers, mechanics, drivers, managers and executives being able to say honestly both EcoBoost Ford GTs finished the 2016 Rolex 24 at Daytona in their competition debut.

Unfortunately, the crew has seen this problem several times before: A wiring defect has rendered a solenoid inert and the electronic paddle shift ineffective, one of several problems that knocked both Ford GTs out of contention long before the sun set on Saturday. On the other hand, by now the mechanics have plenty of experience fixing the problem.

For at least the third time since Saturday afternoon, an offending wiring harness is replaced and Westbrook is given the signal to restart the car. The engine burbles to life, he engages first gear and smartly motors down pit lane to rejoin the race. A few moments later, the ESM Ligier takes the overall win before attention switches to the dueling Corvettes as Gavin sweeps across the start/finish line 0.034s ahead of Garcia, neither car

Eight months after its Calabogie shakedown the Ford GT made its competition debut.

showing so much as a scuff mark that can be attributed to either driver crossing the line between competitive and reckless driving.

Almost unnoticed outside the FCGR pit—and certain television sets in and around Dearborn and Toronto—the Ford GTs cross the line to take seventh and ninth place in GTLM, 32 and 162 laps behind the Corvettes, respectively. Not how the people at Ford Performance, FCGR and Multimatic envisioned things unfolding in their wildest dreams, but hardly unexpected given the EcoBoost Ford GTs had never turned a wheel in competition just 24 hours ago.

"We really wanted both cars running...for us, for the guys, for Ford, to have both cars running there at the end," says O'Gara. "The shift issue reared itself again right before the end on 67, but a quick fix got it running so we could take the checkered flag."

"We approached Daytona with a lot of confidence but at the same time understanding it was our first race. We knew that the timing of all of this was somewhat compressed," says Henry Ford III. "There's always disappointment when you don't win, but I feel good about the future.

"The team had a never-say-die attitude and they were fighting it out until the last minute. That was great to see and having both cars running at the end of the race was a huge accomplishment. We're leaving with our heads high and feeling good about the rest of the season."

Twenty-four hours earlier the Ford GTs lined up last and next to last on the GTLM starting grid, having rolled the proverbial snake eyes during Thursday afternoon's 15-minute qualifying session. The team had arrived in Daytona earlier in the week at the end of a brutal stretch of virtually round the clock work dating back to before the Christmas "holidays."

First had come the push to build a second race car and then prepare two cars for the Roar Before the 24, then the even more intense preparations for the Rolex 24 itself. While the cars ran nearly flawlessly at "The Roar," they were a long way from "Ganassi-ready" to race in the Rolex 24.

For openers, while there were (barely) enough parts to go around and complete two "functional" cars at The Roar, the cars were in what amounted to a "run what ya brung" mode. The team could run the #66 Ford GT with either a stiff or a slightly softer mechanical suspension setup; ditto the #67 car, but there weren't enough springs, dampers and other assorted bits and pieces to enable the two cars to run the stiff or soft setups simultaneously, let alone anywhere in between. So enabling the drivers of one car the chance to sample the other's setup meant swapping the setups on both cars. What's more, given that the two cars were never on the track at the same time with identical setups, overlaying the two cars' data traces was akin to comparing pineapples and rutabagas.

"The car is always evolving, and having two cars makes it that much more challenging to keep them the same," O'Gara explained. "Making sure the parts are the same is everything; otherwise, you might as well have two one-car teams.

"It's making sure they pass tech inspection; it's making sure both cars are equally durable, but also we've got to make sure they're the same performance-wise. We have the same sponsors footing the bill on both cars and we want to make sure they have an equal chance. Needless to say, it's going to be even more of a challenge when we go to France because all four cars have to be exactly the same!"

Compounding the challenges was the fact that, true to his word, in addition to the two Ford GTs Ganassi entered a pair of Daytona Prototypes at Daytona in what was likely the EcoBoost Rileys' swan song. And while the tried and true Daytona Prototypes were again being looked after by the IndyCar crew at Daytona, the two constantly evolving Ford GTs were in the hands of a sports car team evolving from a one-car effort to a full time two-car program.

That crew was still putting finishing touches on cars in the paddock in the lead-up to practice and qualifying. As originally conceived the Ford GT was well under the minimum weight regulations. But with each passing week, it seemed, the cars kept gaining weight—and not because of a poor diet or lack of exercise. Insignificant though it may seem, the weight of the paint needed to turn the cars from grey-black carbon fiber to patriotic red, white 'n blue, coupled with the scores of decals, added up; so too did installing the independent telemetry system IMSA requires on all cars.

So the sleep-deprived mechanics repeatedly had to tinker with the cars' weight, no small task given that the ballast was located under the fuel cell, which had to be removed in order to adjust the weight to get as close to the minimum allowable weight while maintaining an acceptable margin of error.

Nor were those the only adjustments.

74

In IMSA/FIA-think, not only is it best that all the marques in a given class run the same distance between refueling stops, it should take the same amount of time to refuel the different makes of cars so as not to offer a manufacturer or manufacturers an unfair advantage during pit stops.

So far so good but, as different makes of cars have different fuel tank capacities, some juggling is required to ensure cars not only have the same range on a single tank of fuel, but they require an equal amount of time to refuel. The solution adopted by both IMSA and the FIA is to regulate the flow of fuel into the cars during pit stops. Simply put, cars with larger tanks (that otherwise take longer to fill than smaller capacity tanks) are afforded a higher fuel flow rate than cars with smaller tanks. But with the on-board fuel tank capacity subject to adjustment based on, among other things, BoP tweaks to weight, power and downforce, the exercise presents a moving target.

Based on telemetry from the BoP test and The Roar, IMSA initially changed the Ford GTs' fuel capacity from 93 to 98 liters. One small problem: the tightly packaged cars only had room for a 93-liter fuel cell. So IMSA went back to the 93-liter cell but required the team to install smaller fuel regulators in the connection between the pit stand fuel tank and the fuel hose used to refuel the cars during pit stops in order to meet the "delta" time for refilling the smaller tank.

And just to make things more interesting, as Multimatic ramped up the road-going Ford GT's development, various "production car" parts were evolving. In some cases, the race cars were required to keep pace with the updates to comply with the homologation rules. So even as the DP team was spending its time polishing the well-developed EcoBoost Rileys—figuratively speaking, of course—the sports car crew was installing new dashboards on the Ford GTs in the garage.

"I'm still trying to understand how stock a GT car needs to be," said a bemused O'Gara. "I am not sure Ford understands that either. You ask one guy and he says, 'We don't have to run it, it's just Ford wanting to make it look more like the road car.' Then you talk to another guy who says 'You have to run that because it's a production car piece.'

"Well there are plenty of pieces on the car that aren't production car pieces, so I'm not so sure where that line is drawn. But we got it all done and it didn't turn out to be such a big deal as we thought it might be."

Mike O'Gara

Not so the weather at Daytona. Thursday dawned gray and wet, with more of the same on tap for the remainder of the day. Only the brave or those desperate for track time ventured out for the practice sessions, thus most teams and drivers were in a guessing mode when the one hour qualifying session—with 15 minutes for each of the four classes—arrived at 4:25 p.m. With an "out" lap taking every bit of three minutes in these conditions, and flying laps around the two-minute mark, the arithmetic suggested that—at best—any given driver/car would get no more than five qualifying laps.

On the other hand, the wet track offered the chance for an upset by the GTLM cars running on Michelin tires in contrast to the Continental tires mandated for the faster Daytona Prototypes. Under the best of circumstances, the water-logged track would have negated much of the power advantage the DPs enjoy over the GTLMs, but with the added dimension of Michelin's vastly superior rain tires (the 2015 season-ending Petit Le Mans was won decisively by a Michelin-shod GTLM Porsche that simply drove away from the faster DPs on their Continental tires) the GTLM cars had a clear chance to outpace the DPs.

Cognizant of the "danger" of standing out a little too much above the competition lest the BoP police come down on them, FCGR waited until the other GTLM cars posted "target" times before releasing Briscoe and Hand in their Ford GTs. Moments later the sight of a red, white and blue car slithering into the Turn One tire wall flashed on the monitors and shoulders in the FCGR pit slumped.

False alarm. Upon further review, the wayward car proved to be the blue, white and red Ferrari of Team Russia. However, by the time the session had been halted and the Ferrari extricated from the tire wall, time for just two flying laps remained. Briscoe and Hand took to the track, secure in the knowledge that—above all—they were to return to the pits with all eight wheels attached and every body panel in pristine condition.

That they did, notwithstanding Hand's harmless spin in the Bus Stop chicane on his second lap. But when the times were posted the Ford GTs were P11 and P12 in the twelve-car GTLM field at 2:06.758 (#66) and 2:08.440 (#67). (Although the pole-winning Porsche's time of 2:01.408 was more than four seconds clear of the fastest Daytona Prototype, IMSA officials invoked the rule calling for gridding by class when qualifying is held in "variable" conditions.)

Things were somewhat better for Ganassi's "other" program, the two-car Daytona Prototype effort. Per usual, one car featured an all-star team drawn from the Ganassi IndyCar and NASCAR programs with Indy 500 winners Scott Dixon and Tony Kanaan

The Ford GTs splashed their ways to P11 and P12 in GTLM qualifying.

matching up with Daytona 500/Brickyard 400 winner Jamie McMurray and rising star Kyle Larson. The other car boasted a catholic lineup including Priaulx, along with Brandon Hartley (winner of the 2015 WEC LMP1 championship with Porsche teammates Mark Webber and Timo Bernhard), 17-year-old Formula 3 phenom Lance Stroll, and Alexander Wurz, ex-Formula One/WEC driver and current chairman of the Grand Pix Drivers Association who came out of a brief retirement to drive for FCGR.

Although the soggy qualifying times were largely irrelevant, the EcoBoost Rileys showed their age in practice and qualifying, struggling to match the pace of the fastest Daytona Prototypes. The team owner took this into account in a drivers meeting on race day morning with no fewer than 14 driver/sardines in the transporter conference room.

"You're all fast or you wouldn't be here," said Ganassi. "So you don't have to prove anything to me or your teammates. What you do have to do is use your head: at the end of every stint, turn your car over to your teammates in the condition you'd want them to turn it over to you.

"The GT drivers, we know we've got a fast car even though we didn't get to show it in qualifying. DP guys, it's a little different—you gotta drive 10/10ths to keep the leaders in sight. That's understood. Regardless, remember that if a meteor falls out of the sky and hits your car, that's an accident. Anything else is your responsibility."

By 1:30 p.m. the cars were lined up on the grid awaiting the 2:40 p.m. start of the 2016 racing season and, in the case of the Ford GTs, the next step on the road to Le Mans. The mood at FCGR was a mixture of cautious optimism, pragmatism and uncertainty.

"I don't think it really sank in until I sat in the car before the start of the race that, 'We haven't raced a lap in this car,'" said Hand. "'We haven't drafted in this car; we haven't run side-by-side; we haven't had to out-brake anybody yet.'"

The fact that Hand was even thinking about out-braking his competitors testified to the progress made in overcoming one of the car's few shortcomings.

"We never did find a silver bullet for the brakes," Holt explained. "It was just a case of massaging every single component, over and over and, eventually, they become a non-issue."

The FCGR effort was ambitious to say the least.

In fact, apart from minor teething problems, Ganassi's dedicated race car and the development-come race car had run largely trouble-free throughout the testing program; nothing had cropped up that would have prevented them from finishing a race or even required a time-consuming fix that would have knocked them out of contention in a long-distance race.

Not unlike the B-grade movie where the protagonist says, "it's quiet...too quiet" the Ford GTs' remarkable reliability was, at once, a source of satisfaction and cause for concern.

"I'm kind of worried," said Ganassi, only half in jest. "We've run a couple thousand miles, done a 12-hour test and nothing's broken—yet."

"The only thing I know for sure is that sometime in the next 24 hours we're going to say 'Gee, that never happened in testing!'" quipped Nair.

At the start of the race Hand wasted no time moving forward with Briscoe advancing as well, albeit at a slightly more circumspect rate.

"I wasn't trying to be totally easy on the car," Hand said. "I was fairly aggressive, but 24-hour race aggressive rather than Long Beach aggressive where you have an hour and 40 minutes. So I went after it, to be honest, because I wanted to see what it would take; what I could do with it."

A dozen laps into the race Hand found himself within striking distance of the lead. On a Lap 17 restart following a full-course yellow, he slipped underneath the leading Porsche into Turn One to put a Ford GT out front of the 24 Hours of Daytona for the first time since 1969.

"I can say I was the first one to ever lead a lap in the new Ford GT!" Hand grinned. "Can't take that away."

It proved to be the highlight of the race for the Ford GT contingent. No sooner had the Porsche regained the lead than the #67 trickled onto pit lane and made the dreaded left turn into the paddock. The transmission was stuck in sixth gear and no amount of tugging on the paddle shift by Briscoe would change it. Initially the crew swarmed over the car like a hive of angry bees in search of a simple solution to the problem that would enable Briscoe to return to the track quickly and retain the chances of a good finish.

As seconds, then minutes ticked past and hope yielded to reality, the activity turned from feverish to business-like as Weaver, Knostman, Torando, gearbox technician Reid Esquivel and mechanics Shelby Tracy, Trevor Montgomery, Jessica Mace and Phil Binks determinedly effected repairs, secure in the knowledge a win was no longer in the cards.

Soon the #66 car began experiencing shifting problems as well, similar to those that had afflicted its sister car. In both cases the problems appeared to be electrical in nature, as replacing the wiring harness rectified the issue. However, there was more trouble to come in what was destined to become a 24-hour test session, with all hope of victory or even a podium finish gone. Later, the #67 returned to the garage area for an even longer stop to replace a pair of broken dog rings in the gearbox.

Although the root causes of the problems were not readily apparent, a post-mortem revealed that—unbeknownst to FCGR or Multimatic—a supplier had changed the soldering specifications on a solenoid in the gear-change actuator between the Roar Before the 24 and the race itself. Thus had one of the cardinal rules of FCGR (and any professional race team) been unwittingly violated: Never run untried components for the first time in competition.

The case of the broken dog rings was more curious. The failure was traced to a search for fuel economy that resulted in "overly aggressive" engine maps during full-course yellows. In essence, the dog rings failed not because of the strain from gear shifts at 135 mph, but from the engine alternately shutting down and refiring cylinders at 35 mph in the name of saving fuel. And when there are hours of full-course yellow running, as was the

An all too common sight at the 2016 Rolex 24 at Daytona

case at Daytona...

"People think 'Caution! You're barely going around the track,'" said Pericak. "But if you think about it, there's no load on the car so you're loading and unloading the driveline and that's hammering the driveline. When you do it for four hours, that's a lot of hammering—and it's pretty hard to test for four hours of caution!

"On the bright side, the cars ran really well. The pace was good, the fuel economy was good, the drivability was fantastic. The drivers had nothing but good things to say about the race-ability of the car. So those are good things."

Hand, in particular, had plenty of good things to say.

"After my first stint I said to myself, 'That car did really good in its first ever outing as a race car.' One thing I really noticed is that it stopped good. We had some issues with the brakes in the early testing; we were thinking a couple of tests ago, 'Oh man, this could be our major drama.' But I probably outbraked 10 or 12 guys into Turn One in an hour of driving. That says a lot about the brakes.

"The other thing was how well the car drafted. You don't have to be a brainiac to see the car is much lower than the other cars, but that doesn't automatically mean it's going to draft well.

The Ford GTs matched the pace of the Corvettes, Reliability? Not so much.

I mean, with the Daytona Prototype you could be right behind somebody and it wouldn't draft. But with this car you can start to feel the pull about seven car lengths back of the car ahead.

"I was pretty impressed by how good our guys were able to make the car considering the limited resources we had. No joke, we never took the setup we ran at the Roar off the cars; never switched. With all the rain we had for practice and qualifying, we ran the best setup we had from the Roar and never varied. We knew what we had was good and we didn't have to sweat it.

"We need the most work in the low-speed handling department," he continued. "That's something where we spent the least amount of time on. Different parts were still coming in for the race, springs and things that we didn't have throughout testing. So I think from here on out we can start moving toward setups that make better mechanical grip and balance."

To be sure, some of the steps moving forward would also entail revisiting the shift actuator wiring specs, revising the yellow engine maps—and finding some deserted race track where the Ford GTs could run at slow speeds to their hearts'—and dog rings'—content.

Chapter 8
I've Seen Rain and I've Seen
Fire...I've Seen Snow

ROUND TWO OF THE IMSA WeatherTech SportsCar Championship figured to be perhaps the most formidable test the Ford GT would face all season: The Mobil 1 Twelve Hours of Sebring. Moreso even than the 24-hour grinds at Daytona and Le Mans, the half-day race at Sebring metes out extraordinary punishment on every component of a race car—drivers included—owing to the concrete-corduroy surface of the WWII vintage airport runways that make up a considerable portion of each lap.

If it's any solace—and it is to those with a sense of history —Sebring is the only race track on the planet where today's cars and drivers compete on not just a layout similar to the days of yore but, on the pit straightaway, the very pavement traversed by the likes of Juan Manuel Fangio, Stirling Moss, Phil Hill, Dan Gurney and Mario Andretti when they raced at Sebring in the '50s and '60s, not to mention Ken Miles and Lloyd Ruby when they drove their Ford GT40 to victory in 1966.

Prior to the race, FCGR had participated in an open IMSA test at Sebring as well as a private test at Palm Beach International Raceway to confirm that Ford's revised full-course yellow engine mapping strategy was more "dog ring-friendly" than at Daytona. They also tested a revised headlight package to address the drivers' complaints about poor illumination; as well the cars sported reworked cooling ducts in response to signs at the Rolex 24 that the alternator might overheat in the ambient temperatures of a Florida spring—or a European summer.

The tests at West Palm Beach and Sebring went well. Although the drivers remained unenthusiastic about the headlights' illumination, the cars ran without any major hitches during the yellow-mapping test and during the two-day test at Sebring…that is until a coming together between Westbrook and a GTD Porsche damaged the #67's right rear corner sufficiently to bring that car's test to an early end.

On the personnel side of the equation, FCGR welcomed Dixon to its ranks as a third driver on the Westbrook/Briscoe car while, as at Daytona, Bourdais was back with Hand and Müller. Although no official announcement was yet forthcoming about Dixon's inclusion in the 24 Hours of Le Mans lineup, the signs certainly seemed to be pointing in that direction.

"Nothing is confirmed yet," he said. "There are some conflicts between the IndyCar schedule and Le Mans prequalifying and the public scrutineering days at Le Mans…and don't forget I'll be a rookie. But this is an amazing program and the chance to go to Le Mans for my first time on the 50th anniversary of the win with Bruce McLaren and Chris Amon—two Kiwis—would be pretty special."

Although neither car threatened to top the time sheets, the Fords both ran within a half second of the fastest cars during the two days of practice. Come qualifying and the two BMWs easily monopolized the front row of the grid with Bill Auberlen taking the pole with a 1:58.402. Westbrook and Müller were fourth and ninth, respectively, at 1:58.708 and 1:59.053, having focused throughout practice and qualifying on race setup rather than outright speed.

"We're where we've been all week, middle of the pack," Westbrook said. "The car feels really well balanced. We worked hard on that and tried not to react to the changing conditions of this track too much. We're going into the 12 Hours pretty confident."

The Fords each dropped a position at the start before settling in for the first stint. A driver change—with Müller taking over for Hand—contributed to a slow first stop that dropped the #67 Ford back to eighth, just ahead of its sister car by the end of the first hour. Amid occasional spots of rain, however, Müller moved the #66 Ford GT up to third in the second hour with Westbrook advancing to fifth before the heavens opened. First the back straightaway, then the start/finish straightaway, were flooded as drivers tiptoed around the increasingly treacherous track.

Inevitably, one car finally aquaplaned off the road in Turn One and into the tire wall, bringing out a red flag, temporarily halting the race.

The car in the tire wall? That would be the #66 Ford GT.

"I applied the brakes, the left front locked and there was nothing I could do," explained Müller who emerged unscathed from an impact that registered 65 mph on the car's telemetry.

Although the Ford did not escape quite so lightly, the damage was largely confined to its bodywork and right front suspension. After the stricken car returned to the FCGR's paddock workspace on a flatbed truck, the team was prohibited from carrying out any repair work until the race restarted. However, under the watchful eyes of IMSA officials, O'Gara, Weaver, Rees and the rest of the crew were permitted to investigate the extent of the damage and so to have the necessary replacement parts at the ready when they got the green light to work on the car.

Meanwhile, the deluge had resulted in a small lake adjacent to the transporter that threatened to flood the work area. As the team moved some of its equipment to "higher" ground, Bourdais and Briscoe appeared with plastic bags taped around their driving boots to keep them dry—a fashion statement Hand referred to as "sissy boots."

Having advanced another position owing to Müller's

The Ford GTs ran in tandem before Müller aquaplaned off the road.

misfortune, Westbrook was realistically upbeat about the #67 Ford GT's early form.

"The car is very good," he reported. "We overtook a Corvette, a Porsche, a BMW and a Ferrari on the track in pretty much even-up racing, but we also had a couple of bad pit stops… and the windshield wiper could be better. I think fourth is about where we should be pace-wise. It's already a lot better than Daytona."

With the delay approaching two hours, officials gave the crew the get ready signal—Parlett (on her buswoman's holiday from NASCAR) even placed a socket wrench on a bolt, ready to loosen the offending part the instant she got the green light.

The go ahead for the FCGR mechanics coincided with the command for the rest of the field cars to start their engines. Together with Weaver, Rees, Badger, Parlett, Elff and Brooks, Robbie Fast, Steve Namisnak, Kevin Edgley, John Huffman, Brian Beck, Chris Welch, Philip Vars and Adam McKracken efficiently bent to the job, with few wasted motions and even less talk. Once a cluster of mechanics finished their task, they switched to support mode for other, more time-consuming

It was all hands on deck preparing to repair the #66 Ford GT.

procedures—handing tools and parts back and forth to their colleagues like surgical assistants in a hospital operating room. All of 15:32.01 elapsed from the time the OK was given to the time the car rolled out of the tent with Bourdais at the wheel. The fact that the repairs were made while the rest of the field was getting restarted, then circulating under yellow for a couple of pace laps, meant they lost "only" six laps to the leaders.

Still the crash cost the #66 any chance of a strong finish. But the fact the car was out of contention had a silver lining. When the racing resumed and the pavement began drying, FCGR used Bourdais as a guinea pig to determine the optimum time to make the switch from wet to slick tires. The Frenchman pitted for dry Michelins on Lap 89, returned to the track and on Lap 95 turned a 2:10.46 compared to the 2:16.66 Dixon ran that same lap. Hull radioed Dixon to pit for slicks the following lap.

"When I went out on slicks early it was Holy Moses!!!" said the wide-eyed Frenchman. "It took a few laps but once they got going and the track dried a little more it was fine. But it seems like we have a small window of optimal performance for the rain and slick tires."

Dixon took the #67 Ford GT into the lead at the 7½ hour mark.

The battle for the lead was pretty much a Porsche vs Corvette affair, until the seven and a half hour mark when Porsche's Kevin Estre dove inside a GTE Audi into Turn One as Corvette's Magnussen went around the outside of the slower car. As Magnussen turned into the corner, Estre popped out of the other side of the Audi and slammed into the Corvette.

Under the resulting yellow, Dixon took the GTLM class lead—and when the race went green—quickly pulled clear of Ferrari #25, which was initially stuck behind two slower PC cars. In five laps Dixon stretched the lead from 1.6s to 5.7s and then 7.3s while the lead Porsches run nearly 35s behind.

"This was my first time racing in GT competition," says Dixon after handing over to Briscoe a few laps later. "The racing was fairly cut-throat. In DP, if you were faster than the guy ahead of you, he had a tendency to let you through so you could both run your own race. In GTLM it's a lot more competitive.

"We're not that quick on the straights, especially compared to the BMWs, but our setup is very good. We have a good balance in the dry. In the wet conditions there was a little too much understeer, but on slicks we have a good balance. The team has done a great job on the setups, but we're still learning."

Pit stops continued to handicap #67, most notably when Briscoe stopped for fuel and tires during a full-course yellow. As the field prepared to take the green flag a few couple of laps later he roared into the pits reporting something amiss with the rear tires. Small wonder: the tires were inadvertently mixed-up on the pit stop, with the right rear going on the left rear and vice versa.

Although the stop didn't cost him any positions within the GTLM class, Briscoe spent the rest of his stint battling his way through the bulk of the GT and PC fields before pitting for fuel and tires and turning over the car to Westbrook for the final stint. The #67 was back in the pits during a full-course yellow just 11 laps later for its final stop. The team opted not to change the relatively new Michelins in an effort to leap-frog some of the other GTLM cars. The gamble worked—initially—as Westbrook restarted third behind the Corvette of Tom Milner and the Porsche of Earl Bamber with the BMWs of Dirk Werner and John Edwards along with Davide Rigon's Ferrari close behind.

On old tires, Westbrook was powerless to keep Werner at bay on the restart with Edwards coming through as well before the field slowed for another full-course yellow. The caution enabled the Ferrari to close right on the #67's bumper and, when the green flag waved, Rigon bundled Westbrook off track in Turn One. Westbrook managed to keep the Ford GT pointed in the right direction but fell to sixth place before regaining the track only to be gifted a spot when Edwards went off the road after he and Bamber made contact battling for third place.

"Had the race gone green the rest of the way we had a chance at a podium but, as it was, it was difficult to get heat in the tires on the restarts," Westbrook said. "In clean air the car was awesome but we're racing in America and you're going to have yellows. It's that simple. I think we need to have a car that can work the tires a little harder when it's needed.

"That said, to come from where we were at Daytona in the matter of two months and be fighting for a podium in the toughest race in the world is pretty good progress."

"Of course a podium would have been nice," Rushbrook said. "But looking at the big picture, we addressed all the issues that set us back at Daytona and, apart from the crash in some treacherous conditions both cars ran pretty trouble-free. I think the takeaway from Sebring has to be pretty positive."

The weekend of April 15-17 found the Ford GT program at opposite ends of the sports car racing spectrum. The WEC team was making its debut a few miles down the road from its home base in the 6 Hours of Silverstone. The site of a WWII airfield, Silverstone began its motorsports life as a somewhat typical airport circuit turned road course, to wit, flat and lacking in natural features and character. In the intervening half century plus, however, Silverstone has been turned into a thoroughly modern motorsports facility, one that—although it remains for the most part, flat—can take its place among any road course in terms of the challenges it poses to drivers, cars and teams.

Simultaneously, the IMSA team was in Southern California preparing for the Toyota Grand Prix of Long Beach. Run on city streets, the racing surface is second only to Sebring in degree of "roughness" on the IMSA schedule. And with virtually every inch of the circuit bordered by Jersey barriers there is zero margin for error.

Long Beach is also an outlier on the IMSA schedule, as the sports cars play second fiddle to the weekend's IndyCar race. Thus an awkward IMSA schedule consisted of a two-hour practice starting at 7:40 Friday morning then a brief second

The claustrophobic confines of Long Beach were not the Ford GT's cup of tea.

practice at 5:15 p.m. followed immediately by qualifying, with the 100-minute-long race slated for Saturday afternoon at 4:05.

It was a long way to travel to play second fiddle. But Long Beach is IMSA's only opportunity to race in the coveted Southern California market and, if the timetable was disjointed at least it promised the crews what amounted to a relaxed weekend.

The FCGR team spent much of Friday morning's practice experimenting with different Michelin tires and fine-tuning the traction control settings in an effort to maximize the Ford GTs' "launch" out of the Turn 11 hairpin onto the half-mile full-throttle blast down Shoreline Drive. The #67 Ford GT was within half a second of the fastest time of the session when Westbrook saw the fuel pressure plunge…followed by the unmistakable scent of smoke.

Although he quickly brought the smoldering Ford GT to a halt near a marshal's post, it took Westbrook a few moments to wrest a fire extinguisher from a corner worker and began putting-out the fire—his efforts not helped by a marshal inadvertently fanning the flames by vigorously waving a yellow flag.

"Obviously it was supposed to be an easy day," Knostman said. "A session at 8 in the morning and then you don't run again until 5. Then you look up on the big screen and your car's on fire. From the rear bulkhead back, every line, hose, wire and the engine had to be replaced. Not to mention figuring out what caused the problem and what we needed to do to fix it. It was a fairly big task."

Traced to a failed fuel fitting in the firewall, the fire could have been far worse. Although most of the parts were on hand, given that some carbon-charged intercooler pipes had to be overnighted from Indianapolis, there was no rush to make repairs for qualifying. So, having anticipated an easy weekend, the crew got to work rebuilding the business end of the car—a job that would keep them busy until early evening when they knocked off, having done as much as they could without the intercooler parts.

By then, Hand had qualified a disappointing sixth having chosen to run the hard compound Michelins given that IMSA rules stipulate that a car must start the race on the same tires used in qualifying and that Saturday's race was to be run in the heat of the day. But the hard tires were not suited for qualifying, particularly as much of the track was enveloped in shadow—not to mention the fact that Hand severely flat-spotted the left front in a fruitless effort to find the tenth of a second he needed to advance to P5.

Thus the team was left in a conundrum over tires. With the race slated for 4 p.m. on Saturday, perhaps soft tires would be the right choice after all. But to change to soft tires would move them to the back of the grid...alongside the #67 car which, of course, had not even qualified.

"The tires we had in DP sucked, but they sucked equally for everyone," said Hennek. "Michelins are so much better, but we have different compounds, different heat ranges—there's a learning curve with and we're still learning."

In the end, the team bit the proverbial bullet, switched to soft Michelins and started at the very back of the GTLM field.

The WEC team had plenty of its own learning in the first few months of 2016. Having fulfilled their obligations of supplying a pair of Ford GTs to the IMSA program, they could finally begin focusing on their own preparations for the 2016 World Endurance Championship, not least of which was the construction of two

The WEC team made its public debut at the Prologue at Circuit Paul Ricard.

more Ford GTs. While a far cry from the mass production assembly line of Henry Ford himself, the process of building the fourth and fifth Ford GTs went more smoothly than the trial and error method employed constructing the first cars.

The team first conducted private tests at Circuit Paul Ricard in France and Spain's Motorland Aragón. Then came the first official WEC test—The Prologue—at Circuit Paul Ricard, where they ran both cars and then stayed on after the official two-day test to run one car for a 30-hour test—making 22 hours before an "internal component failure" on the engine brought the EcoBoost Ford GT and the test to a halt.

In contrast to the IMSA team, which had been utilizing 2015 IMSA-spec Michelin tires in its testing program and early races, midway through their pre-season testing program the WEC team began utilizing Michelin's 2016-spec WEC tires.

"There had been some good gains made in the tires," said Sole. "We got on really well with them right from the start. In the main, we had been running what the IMSA guys were running and 2016 tires were definitely a step forward."

But as the 2016 Rolex 24 at Daytona proved, testing is one

thing, racing quite another. Particularly for a two-car team that had been little more than a skeleton test car crew less than six months ago. Thus while the 6 Hours of Silverstone not only represented the opening round in the 2016 World Endurance Championship, it was also the coming-out party for the team assembled by Howard-Chappell and based just a few miles down the M-1 in Greatworth Park.

The first of Friday's two free practice sessions found the Ford GTs lapping within half a second of the #71 AF Corse Ferrari and the Dempsey-Proton Porsche, with Johnson posting a 2:02.675 in his first session at Silverstone, marginally quicker than Franchitti's 2:02.887. The problem was the #51 Ferrari lapped at 2:01.067 and, in the second session, knocked another second off its time to wind-up just over the two-minute mark some 0.2s quicker than the #71 Ferrari. Although the Porsche was about a second off the Ferraris' pace, the Fords and Aston Martins couldn't get within two seconds of the Ferraris.

Saturday produced a curve ball, English-style as a dusting of snow greeted competitors arriving at the circuit, leading to the cancellation of the morning practice. And when rain showers dampened the track in the afternoon qualifying session—with

Five months after opening shop, the WEC team prepares for their competition debut.

a car's times based on the average of the fastest laps of two drivers—Rignon and Sam Bird in the #71 Ferrari took the pole with an average of 2:11.900s, more than a second and a half quicker than Richard Lietz and Michael Christensen in the Porsche. However, Pla and Mücke combined to put the #66 Ford third on the grid (2:14.475) while Tincknell and Priaulx were a more circumspect fourth (2:17.387) well ahead of the two Aston Martins and the other AF Corse Ferrari which slithered off the track on its second qualifying run and would start last.

Although Mücke and Priaulx held station behind the #71 Ferrari and Porsche in the opening laps, the Aston Martins of Darren Turner and Fernando Rees were on the move, with Turner passing Priaulx on Lap 32 and demoting Mücke four laps later. After smooth pit stops by the new team, the Fords each moved up a notch when the Porsche encountered mechanical problems; however, the second Aston Martin and the #51 Ferrari were also coming strong.

By the mid-stage of the race the #71 Ferrari was on a lap of its own ahead of the #95 Aston Martin and the #51 Ferrari. The #97 Aston Martin had split the Ford GTs, running two laps down behind Johnson but ahead of Franchitti, the latter of whom had been penalized for stopping for fuel when the pits were closed during a safety car period. Later, Pla was caught out on pit stop strategy when his radio failed and fell behind the #67 Ford as the Ferraris went on to a 1-2 finish ahead of the #95 Aston Martin. With the second Aston Martin dropping out of the race in the final hour, the Fords thus finished P4 and P5 in their WEC debut.

All things considered, it was a successful debut for a team that had been little more than a figment of the imaginations of Holt and Howard-Chappell six months previously, running what, regardless of the IMSA team's experiences at Daytona and Sebring, were effectively brand-new race cars.

"We accomplished what we set out to do," said Sole. "We wanted to run reliably and have two cars finish the race. That's what we were able to achieve, so from our point of view it was a very successful first race."

Franchitti concurred.

"There was a lot of pride in seeing the team come from zero to where we are today, and George deserves a lot of credit for what he's put together," he said. "The team here in the UK at the beginning of December was an empty shop, and we went to Silverstone for our first race and we showed beautifully. It

Fourth and fifth first time out? Mission accomplished.

was an incredible performance: seamless in the pits, the cars ran seamlessly for the race. I don't think we could have done any more.

"We got hosed a little on a full-course yellow—I was coming in that lap with no fuel left, and that was the difference between maybe getting a podium and finishing fourth. But if you'd have asked me before the race I'd have told you if we could get fourth place, I'd be more than happy with that."

Who knows but that a little snow might have done the Ford GTs some good at Long Beach.

Saturday found O'Gara, Goldberg and Hennek in conversation with Michelin technicians John Church and Gary Swingle regarding their race day tire strategy, eventually resulting in a split decision with Hand starting the race on soft tires and, with nothing much to lose after not qualifying, Westbrook going to the grid on a mixture of soft rears and hard fronts.

Meanwhile, with the overnighted parts in hand, Montgomery, Mace, Binks and Esquivel—with a little help from their cohorts who had enjoyed a relatively easy Friday—completed the rebuild of the #67 by late morning, leaving Mace time to work with Westbrook and Briscoe practicing the driver changes with a little more alacrity than they had demonstrated at Sebring. Ominously, at least 50 percent of the time it took her a couple of swings to get door properly latched, the problem exacerbated by the pressurized strut that helped raise the swinging doors. Although re-engineered door latches had arrived at the Ganassi shop from UK as the team was loading-up for Long Beach, there had been no time to install them…

Sure enough, no sooner had the race begun than #66 pitted to have its door re-latched. Compounding the problem, Hand proceeded to exceed the pit lane speed limit, drawing a drive-through penalty. Westbrook, meanwhile, was struggling with the hybrid tire combination.

Still, the Englishman stayed within sight of the leaders by the time it was his turn to hand over to Briscoe. That pit stop exchange went well only for the #67's door latch to come loose on Briscoe's out lap—only to miraculously click closed again

Briscoe and Westbrook repaid their mecchanics' hard work with a fourth place finish.

and remain latched for the duration. Later, however, Briscoe had no choice but to make an unscheduled pit stop owing to a malfunctioning electronic "stuck throttle" switch. Happily, the throttle was not stuck, but the only way to rectify the problem was to "reboot" the system in the pits.

On fresh tires, Briscoe lapped faster than the leaders but rose no higher than sixth place. Then, with just two laps remaining, Porsche's Frederic Makowiecki dive-bombed Tommy Milner's leading Corvette into Turn 11, spinning both cars and promoting the #67 to a fortuitous fourth place. Make that a very fortuitous fourth place. Slowing for the right-hander at the end of Seaside Way on the final lap, Briscoe heard a terrific grinding noise coming from the left front: one of the bolts securing the brake caliper had failed. But with only one more application of the brakes needed before the finish line, he nursed the car to the checkered flag.

Meanwhile, the Hand/Müller Ford came home two laps down in eighth position, but at least had the consolation of Müller setting fastest lap—potentially a mixed blessing in an environment where FCGR didn't want to stand out too far above the madding crowd and risk an unfavorable BoP adjustment heading to Round 3 at Mazda Raceway Laguna Seca in two weeks' time.

Chapter 9
Breakthroughs

NEXT CAME A PAIR of races on two of the world's classic road courses: Mazda Raceway Laguna Seca and Circuit de Spa-Francorchamps in Belgium. While the circuits have much in common, namely a preponderance of fast, sweeping turns and dramatic elevation changes, overtaking opportunities on California's 11-turn, 2.2-mile Laguna Seca are rare. In contrast, the 4.3-mile Spa circuit offers plenty of places to pass—indeed the virtually flat-out run from the La Source hairpin through the daunting Eau Rouge/Raidillon curves and along the Kemmel Straight to the Les Combes S-bend is nearly as long as Laguna Seca in its entirety.

Thus a good performance in qualifying at Laguna Seca would be, if not a necessity, then a leg-up on a good showing in the race. The track also figured to suit the Ford GTs, at least moreso than Long Beach, as the cars' downforce-generating shape would come into its own on the high-speed curves in the infield section and through the critical Turn 6 before the steep climb to the famed Corkscrew turn, as well as through the fast Rainey Curve and Turn 10.

But the Fords had another weapon in their arsenal at Laguna Seca—or to be more to the point, four more weapons—in the form of the 2016-spec Michelin tires that had made their competition debut at the Silverstone WEC race. Whereas the IMSA driving tandems had previously opted for the 2015-spec front-engine car tires, at Laguna Seca they found the latest mid-engine-spec tires built for the Ferrari 488 and Ford GT more to their liking.

Most important of all, however, over the course of two days of practice and qualifying, the Fords ran virtually trouble free—no broken dog rings, no fires, no doors popping open… no time spent diagnosing and fixing "issues;" all time spent on developing well-balanced cars capable of running a strong race pace.

"Everybody involved with the program at Ford, Multimatic, Michelin, Roush Yates, the subcontractors, the vendors, had all been working towards success," said Hull. "One of the most important things was that we went through a full practice and qualifying trouble free. Everything flowed throughout Friday and Saturday. When you can work uninterrupted chasing the race track and developing the setup to run with a fuel load, you can accomplish a lot.

"It was our first time on the new Michelin tires. The WEC team had run these tires at Silverstone and they provided us a lot of feedback and data. But it wasn't until we took to the track for the first time in practice that we were able to begin understanding what all that data meant.

"Michelin only started working with us in late September

Mazda Raceway Laguna Seca was right in the Ford GT's wheelhouse.

with what they believed was a good starting point based on their knowledge and what we were able to tell them about the car. Then they took all the data from the testing and the first races into consideration in developing the new tires…and the car responded well to them."

As well, in addition to being an extended durability run, a post-Sebring test at Virginia International Raceway had afforded FCGR the chance to collect valuable information on "natural" road course setups after having spent the fall, winter and early spring testing and racing at Daytona, Homestead, Sebring and Long Beach, each idiosyncratic in its own way and—ultimately—having little in common with the natural terrain road courses that formed the bulk of the remaining IMSA and WEC schedules, including le Circuit de la Sarthe.

The untroubled practices, the Ford GT-friendly Michelins and the knowledge gleaned from VIR combined to put the Hand/Müller and Briscoe/Westbrook cars near the top of the timesheets throughout practice, which only made the fact that Aseta Corsa Ferrari's Daniel Serra edged Briscoe by 0.079s for the pole (and Müller by 0.248s) all the more disappointing. On the other hand, FCGR had worked on the entire race day package on Friday and Saturday, not "just" outright pace.

Briscoe and Müller held station as the race began, running within a few seconds of Serra's Ferrari, with the Risi Ferrari in fourth, well clear of the nearest Corvette. The first of the leaders to pit, the Fords fell down the order—briefly—but emerged in first and second (with Hand leading Westbrook) once the first round of pit stops was completed. The two Fords continued circling Laguna Seca out front, a few seconds apart and, after the second round of pit stops, remained at the front in a race that had seen three full-course yellows. The resulting fast race pace—and correspondingly high fuel consumption—consigned most cars to a third pit stop for a "splash" of fuel to go the distance.

With about fifteen minutes remaining in the scheduled two-hour race, Hand slowed dramatically in an effort to conserve fuel. Westbrook sailed serenely—if not peacefully—past, both eyes on the road, both ears tuned to "coach" Hull's radio instructions.

"I definitely thought I couldn't save that fuel," Westbrook said. "When Mike gave me the number on the radio I could tell by his voice that he was quite confident…but I don't think I shared his belief."

Perhaps Hull should consider taking up acting in his spare

time.

"Not only did we not know that Richard could save that much fuel, I don't think Richard knew he could save that much fuel!" he laughed. "We worked on it in practice but we hadn't seen him make those numbers in practice. We didn't know if he could do it and maintain his lap times.

"Joey couldn't do it while Richard could. But Joey had more speed, so we wound up on two different strategies. If there had been two more laps of yellow, Joey could have run richer and won the race."

Hand was not alone. One by one the GTLM cars all headed to pit lane, with Westbrook alone making a bid to go the distance on two stops.

"What I realized after the race, what Mike is very clever at, is that he puts the belief in the driver," Westbrook said. "The fact that he trusted me to do it probably made it that bit easier than it was; the fact that he was so sure I could do it, he brought that belief in me and, yeah, we were able to do it."

For an added benefit, as Westbrook braked early entering the tight corners and gently massaged the throttle on exit to save fuel, he was also babying his Michelins, particularly the rear tires: the more gradual the application of the throttle, the less wheelspin; and the less wheelspin, the less rubber left in his wake.

So although "Westy" was still in maximum fuel-saving

The 67 crew greets their car crossing the finish line.

mode—and on Michelins with some 50 laps on them—in the final laps, his pursuers failed to gain any appreciable ground. When the checkered flag waved at the end of two hours—2:01:16.388 to be exact—the #67 Ford GT was 12.5 seconds clear of Alessandro Pier Guidi's Ferrari 488…and the Ford GT had its first win just 351 days after Maxwell's first tentative laps at Calabogie.

"Standing in the pit with the team and with a couple of laps to go I started thinking: 'Is this it? Is this going to be our first win?'" said Henry Ford III. "And I started to get real anxious about those finishing laps. Then Westbrook crossed the line and it was a really powerful moment. It was a prove point that we were really back, officially, and that we were going to be competitive at Le Mans.

"It was really special to be there, along with my brother Stuart. It meant a lot to the family, to the whole Ford organization, to Multimatic, to Chip Ganassi Racing—it was just one of those moments where you get the chance to celebrate and take a moment to reflect on all we've accomplished, all the ground we've covered over the past four or five months. It was really a

Westbrook, Briscoe and friend celebrate the Ford GT's first victory.

special moment."

Having delivered a victory in just the Ford GT's fifth race, Ganassi was in seventh heaven. In typical Chip-think, though, even in celebrating the win he had his eyes on the future.

"Westbrook, man what a job! Briscoe too," he said. "What gets lost is the fact that Ryan kept us in touch with the Ferrari early in the race and saved almost as much fuel as Richard. But you know who their co-driver is at Le Mans? 'The Oil Refiner.'"

That would be Dixon, universally regarded as one of the best drivers in the history of IndyCar racing when it comes to conserving fuel...and who had finally been confirmed as the third driver in the Briscoe/Westbrook Ford GT at Le Mans. Pending, that is, a trip to Paris and his successful completion of a test on the ACO's simulator where he would be introduced to some of the unique aspects of the 24 Hours of Le Mans, including its safety zones and safety cars.

In contrast to IMSA races (and IndyCar road courses) where yellow flags are displayed at the scene of minor accidents and speeds are up to the drivers' discretion, the Circuit de la Sarthe has 35 distinct safety zones. In the case of an accident or a disabled car pulled to the side of the track, flashing signs in the prior safety zone alert drivers that the next safety zone is under caution. They are then required to slow to 80 kph by the time they arrive at the waving yellow flags and flashing yellow lights at the marshals' post immediately before the scene of the accident. They then must travel through the safety zone at 80 kph until they reach the marshals' post at the end of the safety zone where a waving green flag and flashing green light signal they are permitted to resume racing speeds...all the while being monitored by WEC officials observing positional data based on GPS transponders in each of the race cars and prepared to assess penalties of varying severity for exceeding the speed limits.

In the event of a more serious accident, safety cars are dispatched from three different locations—each roughly a third of the way around the circuit. Drivers are required to fall in line behind the first safety car ahead of them until officials deem it's safe to go racing again. Then each safety car pulls off the track at its assigned post and the racing resumes.

In IMSA and IndyCar, of course, the entire field packs up behind a single safety (aka pace) car during a full-course yellow. Thus competitors who were far behind the leader (or even about to be lapped) scurry around to the back of the pack following

Scott Dixon

the pace car, regaining much of the distance they had trailed the leader by the time the race restarts. Not so at Le Mans where the three-safety-car system strives to maintain a semblance of the original gaps. On the other hand, a driver unlucky enough to miss the cut off for a given safety car pack—say he is 10 seconds behind the last car in group A when safety car B pulls in front of him—can lose a third of a lap in the exchange.

Neither system is perfect; each has its plusses and minuses. But the fact is, like any other Le Mans rookie, even a four-time IndyCar champion and a winner of the Indianapolis 500 and Rolex 24 at Daytona was required to familiarize himself with the safety zones and safety cars under the watchful eye of the ACO.

"I don't have a problem with it," smiled the easygoing Kiwi. "It is a different system and it takes some getting used to. Just as a Formula One champion or Le Mans winner has to go through rookie orientation at the Indy 500, it's right that Le Mans rookies should have a good understanding of the safety cars and safety zones. Actually it's pretty cool that you can do it on the simulator. It's not like they can close the roads down at

Le Mans in April and May just for me!"

Even as Dixon was preparing for his Le Mans rookie orientation, the IMSA team's Laguna Seca success was giving the WEC team a little extra motivation when they arrived in Belgium for the 6 Hours of Spa the weekend of May 6-8.

"We've got the monkey off the program's back," said Johnson. "The Ford GT is now a race-winning product, and that's good all around.

"Of course, if you ask any race driver they'll tell you they want to be the ones in the car for the first win. But every single one of them will also tell you they want to be in the car that wins at Le Mans. There's so many different dynamics; but there's no bad aspect about what happened at Laguna Seca."

"I was delighted for the guys over there," said Franchitti. "It was great to see the win. A lot of people don't seem to understand though that we're not running the same car (same BoP rules) in both series, and it's subtle little differences that make a difference in performance. But it was great to have that in America, to show the car's performance. And to win the way they did, with the EcoBoost engine and getting the fuel mileage—yeah massively excited."

Billy Johnson

Although the WEC team had also been encouraged by their debut at Silverstone, they headed to Round Two of the WEC still facing an uphill battle given that, despite the Ferraris' dominating pace in the season opener, there had been no subsequent BoP adjustments to the Ferrari 488 or the Ford GT.

"We all know we've got a tool that can do the business," said Priaulx. "Now we just have to hope the tool is allowed to *do* the business."

Based on the initial evidence, it appeared it would be business as usual for the FCGR Fords at Spa. While the Aston Martin Vantages and Ferrari 488s traded fast laps atop the timing and scoring monitors in practice, the Fords and the Dempsey-Proton Racing Porsche 911 RSR were in the second echelon of the GTE-Pro pecking order, a second (or more) off the ultimate pace.

He may not have been pleased with the Fords' speed relative to the Ferraris and Aston Martins, but Johnson took some satisfaction from the fact that he matched the times of Mücke and Pla on one of the world's most demanding race tracks— despite having never before set foot on Belgian soil.

"Every track where we've tested or raced, I've never been to," he said. "So it's a steep learning curve. But with today's simulation technology you can really get comfortable with the track in a very short time. My first lap here, for example, was right on pace; one of the fastest laps of the weekend. So due diligence and preparation pays off!"

More than just the tracks were new to Johnson. Way more.

"The nuances of racing here (in Europe) have a big impact on your overall performance," he said. "Paying attention to little details that would seem insignificant in IMSA in terms of yellows and pit stops is very important over here with the whole structure of the races. You need to pay attention to those tiny nuances and apply what you learn."

Johnson's observations were not lost on three men named Ganassi, Hull and O'Gara who were on a busman's holiday to Belgium (and in the case of Ganassi, who raced a Formula Ford at Spa in 1978, a return visit). Their objective was to observe the WEC team in action and gain new perspectives on how to approach common challenges.

"We'll see how they race, how they work, how they do pit stops, how their drivers work together and with their engineers," said Hull. "We'll see how a team working with the same cars we work with works to solve problems; in some cases we'll see their problem solvers work on the same problem on the same car in different ways than we would do—just as they did when some of their guys were with us at Daytona and Sebring."

As well, the IMSA-based team would experience, first hand, the subtle and not so subtle "nuances" in the way the FIA-regulated race was run in comparison to IMSA races. After all, the 24 Hours of Le Mans would be run to WEC rules, albeit with a few twists peculiar to Le Mans courtesy of the Automobile Club de l'Ouest.

"We also want to see how the WEC races are run—the pit stop regulations, how they operate at the track," said Hull. "No two sanctioning bodies are the same; there are cultural differences and it's not just a case of IMSA being North American and WEC being European. Chip Ganassi Racing is involved in IndyCar, NASCAR, IMSA and WEC and Global Rallycross. We look at all of them—the way they run their races, the way they administer pit lane—there are differences among all of them. Then you take this sanctioning body (WEC) and add in

Priaulx entertains some interested observers at Spa.

the unique characteristics of Le Mans and you have something different too."

Although the Fords qualified fourth and fifth after the #95 Aston Martin of Marco Sørensen and Nicki Thiim failed to match its practice pace, they still faced a tough battle in the race given that the pole-winning Ferrari was nearly a second quicker than either of the Ford GTs. Nor did a hectic start help matters as—in a bid to win a six-hour race in the first turn—a couple of LMP2 competitors collided and spun as the front row Ferraris sped past. In their wake, the Aston Martins, Pla, Franchitti and the Porsche carefully picked their respective ways through the chaos and completed the opening lap nearly half a lap down on the Ferrari.

In terms of suspense, GTE-Pro style, that was effectively that. The Ferraris loped away in the lead as Pla battled his way past the Aston Martins and eventually handed the #66 to Johnson in third place while Franchitti was forced into recovery mode after a tap from the #95 Aston Martin pitched him into a spin. In contrast to the Aston Martin, which retired as the result of the incident, the stout Ford GT continued and Franchitti worked his way back to fourth by the time he handed over to Priaulx. Later, Tincknell and Mücke battled for third before the latter pitted to repair a loose wastegate connection.

Worse was to come as, after returning to action several laps down, Mücke suffered a punctured tire at upwards of 150 mph in the middle of the fearsome Eau Rouge curve. The Ford GT spun 180+ degrees and ploughed into a tire wall at the crest of the hill, then rebounded into the middle of the track in a shower of shattered carbon fiber bodywork and broken suspension components. Most importantly, the roll cage and cockpit remained intact. Although stunned by the impact, amazingly, Mücke escaped with nothing more serious than a badly bruised foot...great news to everyone in the Ford contingent, none moreso than Franchitti who had relieved Tincknell and was among the first drivers on the scene.

"They said on the radio: 'There's a crash at the top of Eau Rouge,'" he recalled. "I came 'round and I saw a wheel and upright and part of the rear bodywork and I just knew it was Stefan. The first thing I said on the radio was, 'Did you hear from him? Is he OK? Let me know what you can.'

"I didn't know how much they could see on the monitors, so the next time past I told them the safety workers were starting

Priaulx, Tincknell and Franchitti celebrate on the podium at Spa.

to get Stefan out of the car. If you've been racing you have seen crash scenes before and you have a pretty good idea what's going on. It was a good sign they got him out so quickly.

"Then George (Howard-Chappell) came on the radio and told me he was OK, just a bruised foot. So then you think, 'Right that's good news,' and you focus on the job at hand."

When the wreckage was cleared, the full-course yellow ended and racing resumed, the Scotsman needed all the focus he could bring to the job at hand. Having eschewed new tires on the final driver exchange, he found himself defending third place from a resurgent Jonny Adam in the #97 Aston Martin as the clock inched towards the 4 o'clock finish. On fresh tires, Adam was the quicker of the two, but Franchitti had half a minute in hand and was not about to relinquish his position without a fight.

Nor was Nicolas Lapierre in the Signatech LMP2 Alpine, who was simultaneously challenged for the LMP2 class lead by the ESM Ligier of Pipo Derani. The two prototypes closed on Franchitti as the Ford GT plunged through the blindingly fast double left at Pouhon. Into the Campus/Fagnes right/ left Derani dove to Franchitti's right while Lapierre went left as dozens of hearts lodged in dozens of throats in the FCGR garages. To everyone's credit, all three cars emerged unscathed but, hardly had pulse rates returned to double digits chez Ford, than heartbreak descended on the Ferrari garage: With less than 15 minutes remaining in the race, Calado crawled into pit lane trailing the telltale smoke and oil from a blown engine.

As Calado pounded his steering wheel in frustration and the sister Ferrari of Bird and Rigon headed for the win, Franchitti swept past the pits en route to a second-place finish, underscoring the Ford GT's maiden win just a week earlier.

"It was one big team effort," said an enthusiastic Tincknell. "Third place was going to be a great result and then when the Ferrari stopped with a handful of laps to the finish, it was a fantastic bonus to grab second.

"I had a good battle with Stefan [Mücke] before his unfortunate accident. Thankfully, he's okay and that, combined with our result and the Ford GT's win over in States, means the spirits are high in the team. I'm highly delighted with this performance, especially to be heading to Le Mans next month with this result."

"That result was for the team who have worked so hard for these past few months," Franchitti said. "We said we would be pleased to get a podium finish here so to take second place is great."

Sole, was a bit more circumspect.

"The Ferraris had pretty good pace at Spa, as they had at Silverstone," he said. "We certainly couldn't race them. The Astons were a bit closer to us—they've got very good straightline speed—but we were not too bad compared to them from a lap time point of view.

"We ran reliably, but certainly we needed more pace."

Chapter 10
Partners

IN THE FORD MOTOR COMPANY, Chip Ganassi Racing and Multimatic, the Ford GT embodied a tri-cornered partnership among organizations with a diverse range of capabilities; capabilities that sometimes overlapped and, at other times, complemented one another. One characteristic Chip Ganassi Racing, Ford and Multimatic have in common is an unflagging pursuit of excellence.

In that, they were supported by another a pair of partners named Roush Yates Engines and Michelin. In a very real sense, Roush Yates helped made the Ford GTs go down the road, while Michelin made them stick to that road.

ROUSH YATES ENGINES

In 1967, a young mechanic named Robert Yates joined a Holman Moody that had been instrumental in Ford's win in the 24 Hours of Le Mans the previous year and would contribute to additional victories at la Sarthe in '67-'68. Yates, of course would go on to great success in his own right, first as a founder of Robert Yates Racing and, later, Yates Engines. In 2003 Roush Yates Engines was created when Yates joined forces with another legendary racer—Jack Roush—as Ford's exclusive NASCAR engine builders. The partnership produced immediate results when Roush Racing's Kurt Busch won the 2004 NASCAR Nextel Cup and has since gone on to more than 280 wins in NASCAR and, since 2005, IMSA and FIA competition.

Roush Yates Engines partnered with Ford in introducing the 3.5-liter Ford EcoBoost V6 engine into the IMSA series with

Jack Roush, Doug and Robert Yates

Chip Ganassi Racing's Daytona Prototype program in 2014, once again producing (nearly) immediate results when Pruett, Rojas and Marino Franchitti won the 12 Hours of Sebring in just the engine's second race. With four additional wins over the next two seasons (including the Rolex 24 at Daytona), the Ford EcoBoost V6 was a proven commodity—or was at least the most proven component—of the Ford GT as it was designed, developed and prepared for the IMSA WeatherTech SportsCar Championship and the FIA World Endurance Championships in 2016.

"My father wasn't involved in the 1966 Le Mans win, but he was really proud of Holman Moody's involvement with the original Ford GT program," says Doug Yates, who became President and CEO of Roush Yates Engines in 2003. "So we were really excited to start working with the Ford EcoBoost V6 a couple of years ago. It's a real testament to the vision of Ford to spend that time developing the engine so it would be successful in the first year of the Ford GT program."

"We were fortunate in that we were able to do a lot of testing ahead of time; that was one of the luxuries that the car didn't have because you can't go track testing until you have the car," says Jon Giles, General Manager of the Roush Yates Performance Engine Group. "We had engines and we had a great place to start with the Ford EcoBoost engine we raced in Daytona Prototypes for a couple of years. From there we just kept tuning on it."

Nor did they have to reinvent the fiendishly complex electronic interfaces with the gearbox and other systems.

"The integration of the electronics of the engine and the gearbox talking to one another, the gearshifts...that side of it is often a massive hole you can quickly fall down if you're not careful," said Sole. "But that was pretty good from Day One as well, so we were able to get out and get running without having to sort out electrical bugs."

But while the architecture of the IMSA GTLM/WEC GTE-Pro EcoBoost V6 was fundamentally the same as that which powered Ford's Daytona Prototypes, the accessory equipment required extensive modifications and, in many cases, wholly new design in order to perform at optimal levels.

"There were a lot of changes that were driven from the package, from the buttresses to the turbos and all the plumbing, so all of that was new," says Mark Rushbrook. "The turbo sizes were different because with the DP we were running at a higher power than what we are allowed to with the GT engine.

"We wanted to (re)size the turbos and then optimize the airflow because with different power levels you've got different airflow through the engine. So even though it was, in theory, a carry-over and proven engine it was a different application that required a lot of re-design, re-engineering to optimize its performance at those power levels and that package."

Adding to the challenge is the fact that the Ford GT's "packaging" is downright claustrophobic, to say nothing of a royal pain for mechanics.

"The GT engine component is a very tight package, with the semi-stressed engine configuration, finding mounts that would integrate into the chassis and providing adequate plumbing routing was quite demanding," says Giles. "Our designers worked closely with the folks at Ford and Multimatic from the early stages of the project to optimize the design configuration. When you look inside there is no extra space for anything.

Tyler Reese and Wade Riesterer

"It is such a tidy package. We're focused on the reliability anyway—if you have to service any part of the car during the race at Le Mans and it's going to take you any period of time, it will put you out of contention. So anything they could do with the packaging to keep the profile of the car as slippery as possible—that was job number one."

Working in concert with the designers and aerodynamicists, the engineers optimized the airflow around the car to enhance the turbochargers' intercooler efficiency. As well, given the space constraints, in some cases what had been "soft" water and oil lines had to be run as "hard" lines in the Ford GT.

"Our oil filtering system had to be unique and compact to fit in the space provided," Giles says. "It was designed specifically for the Ford GT application. We definitely did not go to the parts bin!"

Although Ford and Roush Yates turned to carbon fiber for key components like the intake manifold and cam covers, given the homologation restrictions they were severely restricted in their ability to change the fundamentals of the EcoBoost. However, given the stream of BoP adjustments to the boost curves on both the IMSA and WEC side, Ford and Roush Yates were kept plenty busy reacting to the boost changes and re-optimizing the engine management system.

"With the ever-evolving BoP, they kept giving us new boost curves and our calibration team went right back to the drawing board, always trying to optimize everything we had in the engine to give the drivers that response they were looking for," Giles says. "Particularly because you're running against guys like the Corvette (and in WEC Aston Martin) where you just plant your foot and you'll have instant response."

While the frequent BoP adjustments kept the folks at Roush Yates and Ford Performance technicians and engineers on their toes, happily they did not have to go back to their proverbial drawing boards to deal with reliability issues. The engine's durability was first proved in 24-hour tests back at Ford, in the very dynamometer cell (17G) that was used for the GT40 engine in the '60s. The team was led by engine engineer Dave Simon, who was instrumental in adapting the Ford EcoBoost production engine to the rigors of racing. So much so that, during all the testing and racing miles logged by the IMSA and WEC teams, there was only one significant glitch with the power plant.

"We have not had any engine failures in the races that have caused any issues," says Rushbrook. "We did see a failure at the Paul Ricard test that was manufacturing-related to one of the internal components, but we understood what it was when we diagnosed it and made sure it never happened again."

Some of the reasons it never happened again are named Craig Ashmore, Phillip Vars, Charles Vogel, Adam McMaster and Wade Riesterer, the Roush Yates Engine's Technical Team embedded in FCGR's IMSA and WEC teams to monitor the EcoBoost's real-time telemetry.

"We're the first line of defense," says Riesterer, Technical Manager of the Roush Yates Engines Sports Car Program. "If we see a car's water temperature approaching our operating limits, for example, we'll alert the race engineer who, in turn, radios the driver. Maybe he's been drafting another car a while, so now he'll pull out of the draft for a lap or two to get more fresh air into the radiators.

"We monitor the boost pressure to ensure it's within the limits defined by the IMSA and FIA BoP. We also use live telemetry data and driver feedback to adjust traction control. For example, as the rear tires wear and track conditions change over the course of a stint, we may suggest the driver switch to a more or less aggressive traction control strategy to continually optimize car performance."

Hunched over adjacent laptops in the FCGR pit and garage you'll find vehicle dynamicists John Kipf (Ford) and John Leveille (Multimatic) and, at WEC races, Matt Johnson (Ford) and Vince Libertucci (Multimatic). As the Roush Yates engineers monitor the EcoBoost V6, so the vehicle dynamicists are responsible for the care and feeding of the Ford GT chassis—watching how tire wear and subtle adjustments to the dampers and aerodynamics, for example, affect the cars' performance.

"It's something of an exercise in reverse engineering," Kipf observes. "Knowing the preferences of each driver, the compromises we have to make with two or—in the long distance races—three different drivers in the same car, and working with the race engineers to tailor the car's characteristics to their strengths."

As well, Kipf and his colleagues record how changes in the chassis and aero setup, track and weather conditions correlate with the Ford and Multimatic simulation programs. Following every test and race weekend, they download the new information into the simulations' data banks in an ongoing effort to close the gap between the virtual reality of the simulator and the real world.

Michelin brings some 6,000 tires to Le Mans.

MICHELIN

"Whether it's an Indy car, a stock car, a sports car or even a rallycross car, the only thing connecting them to the race track is four small patches of rubber. As a team, I'd like to think some of the things we learn in one discipline we're able to take and apply to our other programs."

Those were Chip Ganassi's words during a press conference announcing his induction into the Motor Sports Hall of Fame the day before the racing debut of the Ford GT in the 2016 Rolex 24 Hours of Daytona. And while he was talking about the mindset behind his team's participation across the motorsports spectrum, Ganassi put his finger on one of racing's ultimate maxims: No matter how powerful its engine, how efficient its aerodynamics, how effective its suspension, how talented its driver, 100 percent of every race car's performance is transmitted to the racing surface through its tires.

When Ford decided to race the Ford GT, there was little doubt they would do so on Michelin tires. Apart from the Aston Martin WEC program's association with Dunlop, the manufacturers in both the IMSA GTLM and WEC GTE-Pro classes all partnered with Michelin. Understandably so. After all, Michelin technical partner teams claimed nine of the 10 GTLM class victories and 28 out of a possible 30 podium places in the 2015 IMSA WeatherTech SportsCar Championship, not to mention 18 consecutive overall victories at the 24 Hours of

Le Mans.

Impressive to be sure, but the words "technical partner teams" are even more significant. The relationship between Ford and Michelin would go much deeper than "just" supplying racing tires to the IMSA and WEC Ford GT teams. The partnership encompasses developing tires for the full range of vehicles in the Ford Performance domain, including Ford GT road car of course, but also the Mustang GT, Shelby GT350 and 350R, F-150 Raptor, Focus RS and ST and Fiesta ST.

As for the Ford GT, Michelin was involved, if not from the get-go, in the formative stages of the road and race cars. As early as 2014, Michelin's North American Motorsports Director, Chris Baker participated in meetings with Multimatic, Roush Yates and Ford Performance developing a strategy for the Ford GT racing program.

"At that point the Ford GT only existed as a simulation on a hard drive somewhere," Baker says. "We talked about basic things like, 'OK, we're building the car around the FIA GT rules. Are we taking full advantage of the tire sizing allowed by those rules? You've got a roughly 14″ x 28″ box that you can put the rear tires in and similar for the front axle, so what are we doing to make sure we are taking full advantage of that?'

"It starts there. Then there are tons of other things you can do once you have, as we do, a variety of solutions to offer. The simulation work gets you in the batter's box, it might even get you to first base…"

Ford's Kevin Groot and Mark Rushbrook with Chris Baker

John Church talks tires with Dirk Müller.

Going further requires real world experience, however, so Michelin technicians were on the ground from the moment Scott Maxwell took the Ford GT for its first laps at Calabogie through the FCGR pre-season testing, every race weekend and every in-season test. Specifically, Michelin technicians John Church and Gary Swingle were embedded with the IMSA team while Sylvain Derain was part and parcel of the WEC program.

Although Michelin could (and would) produce tires designed specifically for the characteristics of the 2016 mid-engine Ford GT and Ferrari 488, as with any scientific process, they started-off with knowns.

"Your testing program, even your simulation program, begins with a stable, known solution from the analytical point of view," says Baker. "Then your empirical program begins with a well-known, simple solution. Don't make it complicated: Work on the car first and then when the car gets closer to where you want it to be, then you start looking at the potential for types of powerful tire solutions."

Once the FCGR testing program was under way, Michelin began offering more "powerful" options, including the tires used by the mid-engine Ferraris 458s in the 2015 IMSA campaign— but also those in use by the front-engine BMWs and Corvettes and the rear-engine Porsches. Although the construction and rubber compounds of tires for a front-engine car differ from those of mid-engine and rear-engine cars, Michelin strives to ensure its tires all have the same ultimate performance potential regardless of the chassis. And, in offering the drivers and teams a wide range of options, not only was Michelin gathering a similarly wide range of empirical data, it was also emphasizing the basic tenets of its racing program.

"This is danged near a religion in our company: All of our partners can look at anybody else's stuff," says Baker. "If you want to try Porsche solutions on the back of your Ferrari, have at it brother. What you're probably going to learn is that they don't work! But if you think the Porsche guys have something you don't have, step on up and try 'em. Then when you learn what we've told you is the truth, you can go back to the stuff that works on your car.

"We're not favoring anybody. We're developing solutions that are appropriate for those chassis and if somebody wants to try to reach out and try something else...and the BMW guys have been really good at that. They'd try anything."

Curiously, the FCGR drivers initially preferred the tires Michelin had developed for the Corvette—at least for the Ford GT's front tires. Although that may seem counter-intuitive, if not downright bizarre, it underlines how dominant a role tires play in a driver's "feel" for a race car. Quick: What did Ryan Briscoe, Joey Hand, Dirk Müller and Richard Westbrook have in common?

"Most of them were coming from either Corvette or other type cars, not necessarily a mid-engined type car," says Church. "I think they found themselves in a familiar area with that front tire. They were toying with which way to go and it was a hard decision. We opined on what we thought was the right way to go and they ended up making a different choice for front tires for the first half of the season."

However, the second half of the season—or at least the part that began at Silverstone and Laguna Seca—saw the Ford GTs take a different tack. Based on nearly a year's worth of testing, along with the data from the Rolex 24 of Daytona and Mobil 1 Twelve Hours of Sebring, Michelin produced different spec tires for the 2016 WEC campaign, tires that made their competition debut in the WEC season opener and the fourth round of the IMSA WeatherTech SportsCar Series; tires that were adopted by both FCGR and the Ferrari teams on both sides of the Atlantic.

"Inputs from the Ferrari teams and the Ford development

work informed the 2016 WEC solutions, which were introduced at Silverstone and Laguna Seca where, interestingly enough, Ford won," said Baker. "At this time the Ford solutions and the Ferrari solutions are exactly the same. That's not to say that at some point in the future that we would not evolve to a Ford- or Ferrari-specific solution...if we deem that necessary."

Equally important, although Church, Swingle and Derain wear the same Michelin blue and gold uniforms as their counterparts like Lee Willard and Clayton Pjorlie (Corvette), Michelle Phillips (Risi Competizione), Brian Hightower (Porsche N.A.) and Tony Coleman (BMW Team RLL), what happens at FCGR stays at FCGR, just as what happens at Corvette, Risi, Porsche and BMW stays at Corvette, Risi, Porsche and BMW... up to a point.

"At any race, we'll have a bunch of guys running around acquiring data," says Baker. "The only people who know everything about every car, and who will have the consolidated view of our situation at any one time, will be guys like Kim Paine, our North American technical director, Robby Holly, our operations manager and championship leader, or me. We will know everything about every car: the individual camber settings, the hot pressures they're running, the starting cold pressures, even race strategy.

"We have a central braintrust that is cognizant about what's going on for all of the cars from prototype through GT, and that's limited to a handful of people.

"If there is a trend emerging—let's say for example we see the track surface temperature is evolving in the direction of the frontier between our cool temperature and our medium-medium across all chassis...if we see empirical performance, lap times, temperatures, that sort of thing that we're moving toward the performance frontier, then the central braintrust can send a signal to everyone to say 'Alert: We're seeing some evolution across all chassis: Be ready.'

"That's the value of having all the information in the hands of a few folks, who can then provide direction and orientation to each individual pair of engineers in the pits."

Indeed, while the name emblazoned across their paychecks may read MICHELIN, from the perspective of the embedded members of the teams, there's definitely healthy competition.

"John (Church) and I work on Ford, Lee and Clayton work for Corvette," says Swingle. "We're all with the same teams all year long, and we have competition between each other. Each of us wants to see our cars win; there's certainly pride there as well."

Although the partnership is still in its early days, midway through their first season together a considerable amount of mutual respect has already developed between FCGR and Michelin.

"Working with Ganassi you immediately understand they are professional; they've got all their bases covered," says Church. "Some of the first things I noticed is the team *likes* each other; everybody knows their role; they know how to do this. It's not their first rodeo, so we're both learning the good from each other's experience. Quite a few of their guys have IndyCar experience. The things they've learned about tires qualifying at 225 mph that are so important for them to monitor—we're learning from them and their tools how better to exploit our tires.

"At the same time they're looking to learn from us how far we take grip levels, what we do with different options, how far we push the envelope because we have different competitors around us—they see how we take a very high interest in very scientifically setting pressures, watching conditions such that when these guys hit the track they have tires that are pressured correctly...so it's a great experience working with them so far."

"We're just starting with Michelin, scratching the surface," says Hull. "Their attention to detail; their engagement in the entire process; their willingness to unselfishly help; their willingness to help us with our product that utilizes their product by listening to what's going on, by watching what's going on, by learning from us as to what will make our car better—it's what you want to see in a partner.

"They do all the right things. It isn't repetition for them: it's always realization. They continue to try to make themselves better, their product better, and for them it's their life's work. It's not like: 'We won Le Mans 18 straight times, now let's go do something else.' They're into this thing to win again and again and again. And you know what? That kind of fits us!"

Chapter 11
Welcome to Le Mans

THE CIRCUIT DE LA SARTHE that welcomed the two-pronged Ford Chip Ganassi Racing team the first week of June is at once very different from and similar to that conquered by the original Ford GT40s.

Where the circuit's legendary Mulsanne Straightway stretched uninterrupted for 3.5 miles in the days of Henry Ford II and Carroll Shelby, in the name of safety a couple of medium-speed chicanes were added in 1990 to break up "the Mulsanne" into three shorter sections. Similarly, the gentle curve beneath the iconic Dunlop spectator bridge just after the start/finish line that Amon, McLaren and their colleagues approached at upwards of 180 mph is now bisected by a tight chicane that knocks 100 mph off the speeds. And what was once a terrifying blast along gently meandering country roads from Arnage Corner through Maison Blanche to the start/finish straightaway has been supplanted by a purpose-built section of high speed swerves familiarly known as the Porsche Curves (technically the Porsche Curves, the Karting Esses and the Virage Corvette) leading to the successively tighter Ford and Raccordement chicanes.

And yet, just as in the '60s (and the '50s, 1949, the '30s and '20s for that matter) the circuit is still largely comprised of public roads used by cars, trucks, motor- and bicycles most of the year; roads that alternately run laser straight between Le Mans and Tours, rise, fall, twist and turn through forest and farmland, and split a massive grandstand and pit complex; roads that bear the everyday markings of turning lanes, passing and no passing zones; roads that, despite the ACO's best efforts, start the month

Edsel B. Ford II returns to hallowed ground.

of June in a dirty, dusty state and which only truly "rubber-in" several hours in to the 24-hour race itself.

And at 8.469 miles, each lap of the contemporary Circuit de la Sarthe still packs just about every challenge imaginable to car and driver alike…

"Because half of it is on public roads it's not like you can test here year around, so there's a special moment in that it's a once a year kind of thing," said Tincknell. "In terms of the actual track itself and the layout, it's got a bit of everything so you've got to have a versatile car and a versatile driving style. You've got long straights where you want low drag and you've got the superfast Porsche Curves where you want as much downforce as possible; you've got tight, twisty chicanes with big curbs and you've got tight corners at the end of very fast bits, so you've got to be good on the brakes. It's a real all 'round test which I think is great and it's what they wanted when they first came up with it: an all 'round test for the cars to prove they're best in all different aspects, and that's still the case today."

The FCGR team was reasonably confident the Ford GTs would be up to the unique challenges of the 24 Hours of Le

The 24 Hours of Le Mans: a not so quiet drive through the countryside.

Mans. After all, they seemed to have put the teething problems of Daytona and Long Beach behind them in the wake of the WEC squad's smooth Silverstone debut and second place at Spa, not to mention the IMSA team's Laguna Seca victory.

"I think a problem-free weekend was important for Laguna Seca," Briscoe said, "but I also think it was important in preparation for Le Mans. We needed to have a clean weekend where everything was working the way it was meant to. Honestly, we wanted to win Daytona, Sebring, Long Beach— all the races—but it was all in preparation for Le Mans. We hadn't had a clean event, so it was important—even if we didn't win—it was good to have a good solid weekend with everything working the way it should.

"You never know how a race will turn out. At the end we had a good strategy and no mistakes, it worked out and we won. But I think more importantly, everyone did their job, the car did its job and we came away feeling pretty good. We went into Laguna thinking, 'I'm not sure we're ready for Le Mans.' We left Laguna saying, 'You know what? I don't know if *ready* is the right word, but we felt a lot better about Le Mans.'"

FCGR's subsequent test of the Le Mans aero package at Monza, Watkins Glen and Road America had gone smoothly, enabling the drivers and engineers to focus on progressing with chassis and aero setups for Le Mans rather than twiddling their thumbs as mechanics dealt with mechanical problems.

"We're happy with where we are at this point," said Sole. "We've got pretty good reliability although with a brand-new car I don't think you can ever be confident. Le Mans with a car you've been running for two or three years, and you know every nut and bolt, all its strengths and weaknesses, is daunting enough, but a new car is always a bit more challenging.

"But I think we feel we've got a reasonable setup on the car, and a reasonable handle on reliability and so we're in a reasonable position."

Even Mücke's thunderous crash at Spa had its silver lining for, apart from that bruised foot, he emerged from the wreckage intact. Indeed, while many a body panel and suspension component had to be replaced, the Ford GT's tub withstood the impact and, after the mechanics put in more long hours at the Northampton shop, the car was ready for the Monza test.

In fact, rather than undercutting his confidence the accident boosted Mücke's outlook in a counterintuitive fashion best understood by racers.

"The tire barriers absorbed a lot of the impact and the car was very strong," he said. "The tub was not badly damaged; we repaired it and brought it to here to race at Le Mans. It's never nice to have a big crash like that, but it is good to know the car is strong and you feel confident it will protect you if something bad happens again."

Nevertheless, an assortment of technical, procedural and psychological challenges loomed. In addition to conducting tests at Watkins Glen and Road America, the IMSA team had devoted long hours at the Indianapolis shop packing shipping crates with upwards of 30,000 pounds of parts ranging from spare bodywork, exhaust systems, gearboxes and steering wheels to the computers and printers needed for more than three weeks of testing, practicing, qualifying and racing in a foreign country.

And for all the team's success, recent and otherwise, the confidence they brought to the Circuit de la Sarthe was tinged with a sense of unease.

"We had done overseas IndyCar races where we had to assemble equipment and things, but we had never been in a situation where you were going to be there for 23 days. So what do you pack?" says Goldberg.

"We were working side-by-side with the UK team for the first time. What could we expect from them? The Indianapolis-based team had never dealt with the FIA or the ACO, so there was anxiety among the entire group from truck drivers to the managers on how it was going to play out. Then there was the intimidation of walking into a place and knowing you're going to be there for that long; not only that, the history of the place."

The first few days unloading and setting up were challenging. Loaded with parts and essential—and heavy—equipment like engine hoists, the overseas crate was deposited about a mile from the pits. Thus the crew had to drive a forklift back and forth to transfer the material to the garage.

There were also updates to be installed on the cars, a new aero body kit for example, but also FIA-specific items including a data blogger, leader lights and an assortment of details to bring the cars into compliance with the nuances of the FIA regulations.

"IMSA has adopted the FIA rulebook, so our cars have to be the same," explained O'Gara. "But what IMSA and the FIA haven't agreed on is what data logging system to use to make sure we're complying with all of those rules. So dimensionally, the brakes, the turbos—that's all the same whether it's Laguna Seca or Le Mans. It's all the electronics on board to measure all the stuff that's different. So the car radios had to change—they operate on different frequencies; the telemetry system that sends all the information back to the FIA is different from what IMSA uses. For the IMSA races we have number panels in the doors that display the car's position in the running order; WEC cars have three lights with one lit if you're in first, two if you're second and three for third place.

"A lot of the thrash was getting all the electronics in the car and the wiring looms because it's not just a small wiring thing: there are sensors all over the car the system has to connect to. The biggest thing we had to do was get that system in the cars and make sure it worked."

And preparing the cars for WEC specs was only half the battle. There was a bewildering array of unfamiliar pit equipment to be assembled while the team familiarized itself with "foreign" pit stop procedures and regulations governing their actions on pit lane and in the garages.

For example, at IMSA races the team works from a mobile

The IMSA crew gets acquainted with WEC pit procedures.

pit stand located hard up against the pit wall, with the pit crew jumping over that wall to service the car on pit lane. At Le Mans (as at other WEC races), teams work out of permanent garages along pit lane with the engineers and managers sitting in the back, separated from the main garage by a plexiglass wall and banks of monitors. Immediately behind the garage, under an awning, is an area where mechanics and technicians conduct a myriad of tasks ranging from preparing and maintaining spare parts to small-scale fabrication, caring for and feeding the drivers' helmets...and heating tires. Unlike in IMSA, where tires must be installed on cars at the ambient temperature, WEC rules allow teams to warm tires in furnaces behind the garage in order to be at optimal operating temperature when they are bolted onto the car during pit stops.

As well, there are significant differences when it comes to routine servicing of a car in the pits during IMSA and WEC races. For example, IMSA allows simultaneous refueling and tire changes while WEC crews are prohibited from changing tires (or doing any other work on the car apart from cleaning the windshield) until refueling is complete. And where IMSA allows a pair of two-person teams (with one air gun for each pair) to change tires, WEC tire changes must be performed by two crewmembers using a single air gun.

In the event repairs are required during an IMSA race, the driver slowly pilots the car back to the team's transporter in the paddock where work commences; in WEC events the driver stops in front of the garage, the crew jacks the car onto a rolling metal platform called a skate, and pushes it into the garage where the work is performed.

If that all sounds bewildering, imagine performing pit stops under the pressure of race conditions to a crew ingrained in IMSA procedures...

Thus when pre-qualifying practice got underway on June 5, the IMSA side of the garage was as focused on gaining familiarity with the pit and garage area procedures as with making their two cars (now numbered #68 and #69 in deference to the WEC team's #66 and #67) go fast.

"The test days were all about getting used to how everything runs and developing a rhythm," says Hennek. "By the end, everything was working really well. It was like: 'Hey, the car comes-in-goes-on-the-skates-comes-back-into-the-garage-tires-go-off-back-in-the-heater-bolt-on-new-tires-drivers-talking-we're-doing-the-changes-got-that-done-roll-it-back-out...and go!'

By no means did things go perfectly. IndyCar's doubleheader race weekend at Detroit prevented Bourdais and Dixon from taking part in the session (the good news for Bourdais if not Ganassi, is the Frenchman won Saturday's race in the KVRT entry), while a leaky fuel cell limited Hand and Müller to just 43 laps of practice in Ford GT #68 (compared to 76 circuits run by Mücke, Pla and Johnson in Ford GT #66).

And there were some slip-ups in the pits.

"One time I counted six ACO officials in our pit box trying to talk to Brett. I told him on the intercom, 'We've just done something horribly wrong,'" Goldberg laughs. "But we needed to do those mistakes; we needed to get them out of the way, learn from them and move on.

"In IMSA, with full-course yellows and wave arounds, you can recover from a penalty pretty easily. But with the WEC regulations with slow zones and split safety cars, no full-course yellow, no pack-up, no wave around—this is a whole different world.

"With this being our first time at Le Mans, as much as you'd like to do your pit stops as fast as the Aston and Corvette guys, there's a learning curve. I told the guys if we lose one second on a pit stop I don't care. That's not going to lose us the race. If we get a drive-through penalty that's 30 seconds—that's hard to come back from. One second is not the end of the world. 30 seconds? That hurts. Get another 30 seconds...

"The car is the car, the setup on the car—there's only so much you can do there."

Fortunately, the cars' setups were pretty good. Briscoe, Westbrook and Dixon led the way for the Ford contingent at 3:56.039, just ahead of Johnson, Mücke and Pla with the other two cars about a half second slower. The Ford GTs were by no means fastest—the quickest Corvette turned a 3:55.122 and the fastest Porsche a 3:55.402 while the AF Corse Ferrari checked-in at 3:55.900 some 0.2s quicker than the best Aston Martin—but the FCGR drivers were pleased with their cars' balance.

"All the drivers said, 'Wow that's the best car we've ever had from a balance point of view around here at Le Mans,'" said Mücke. "That's very promising. It gives you a very good feel."

Tincknell seconded that emotion.

"We ended with a very consistent, driver-friendly car," he said. "The rear was very stable, with just a little understeer. If you had to drive that for 24 hours you'd be very happy.

"Of course we have a little bit of time to come, but if we keep tweaking and tweaking during the week, I think we can get there. A second around here is not that much when it's close to a four-minute lap."

So with ten whole days between the test and the race, it was vacation time for the crews, right? Guess again. Yes, most everyone on the team got a couple of days to relax, visit Paris, tour the Normandy beaches or in other ways experience France. Binks, for one, spent some time consorting with the enemy...namely his father Dan, highly respected crew chief on the Corvette C7.R driven by Magnussen, Garcia and Ricky Taylor—and one of the Corvette Racing team members who gave the victorious FCGR team a rousing cheer when the Ford GT pulled into pit lane at Laguna Seca.

"It was good to get away from the track, spend a little time with my dad," said Phil, who was named after his grandfather who worked with a couple of guys named Shelby and Miles on the Ford GT40. "Of course we talk some racing, maybe needle each other a bit, but mostly we talk about family and other things."

Had Dan and Phil Binks wandered into the same restaurant as

Phil and Dan Binks

Larry Holt, they might have witnessed an interesting conversation between the man from Multimatic and a local resident who paid Ford Chip Ganassi Racing a supreme compliment.

"I was having dinner in town and this guy cornered me and said something pretty significant," Holt says. "He made some derogatory comments about some of the programs that have come and gone and he said the thing that he likes, the thing that we like—the people of Le Mans and the French in general—is that Ford respects Le Mans.

"I think that's a true statement. Everything we're doing really does respect this race. I didn't make that up. That's some French guy I met in a bar."

There was also a bit of time to relax each evening after the crew left the track. Rather than staying in yet another motel or hotel, the crew was lodged in several private homes in and around the circuit. That made a world of difference.

"It was way better staying at a house," Mace says. "You had more freedom. Our hosts made dinner every night, so there were always leftovers. If you got hungry in the middle of the night you could get something good instead of going to a vending machine in the hotel lobby. It was really nice because you had a common area where you could sit and talk, relax. There was room to spread out; we had room outside where we could get some exercise throwing a football around, it was way better than staying in hotels all around.

"The guys I was with all worked on the 68 car and I was on the 69 car. Normally, you don't really pay attention to what the other car is doing unless you're having the same problems. So I listened to every issue they had each day and some of the stuff they ran into. Even though you're the same team, you are so focused on the car you work on that you don't know what's happening with the other guys."

While it may not have been all work and no play, there was still much to do to prepare for the official scrutineering in the city center the weekend prior to the race, to say nothing of official practice and qualifying a few days later.

Apart from a few minor safety issues (e.g. the amount of tension on the drivers' door window safety netting) the city center scrutineering went well, to the relief of the teams and the entertainment of tens of thousands of aficionados in attendance. There were, however, two notable absentees: Sebastien Bourdais and Scott Dixon. A deluge at the Texas Motor Speedway

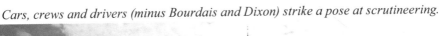

Cars, crews and drivers (minus Bourdais and Dixon) strike a pose at scrutineering.

forced IndyCar organizers to postpone the race from Saturday until Sunday (and eventually, to reschedule it later in the year), meaning the two drivers didn't arrive in Le Mans until Monday afternoon—fortunately they were given dispensation for missing scrutineering by an accommodating ACO, no doubt willing to cut the "local guy" and the IndyCar champion some slack.

With the cars OK'd, the late arriving drivers duly checked in—and after a team dinner party hosted by Sebastien and Claire Bourdais at their home a few blocks from the city center—FCGR girded itself for The Week from Hell, one that began with preparing for practice and qualifying running from 4 p.m. through midnight Wednesday and Thursday, followed by a "quiet" day of final preparations on Friday. That was but a prelude to a sadistic race day schedule that saw the pre-race warmup run from 9:00 to 9:45 a.m., some six hours before the start of a 24-hour race. With crews rising early Saturday morning in order to be at the track for the warm up, it would be well over 36 hours before crews whose cars went the distance in the race could even think of going to sleep on Sunday evening.

And it's not like they headed into race weekend well rested. Preparations for practice and qualifying continued with much time, energy and no small degree of wailing and gnashing of teeth in the Ford GT garages devoted to the fueling rigs, specifically the fuel restrictor—the flange connecting the fueling hose to the pit side fuel tank that regulates the rate of fuel flowing into the car during a refueling stop. In FIA- as in IMSA-think, not only is it best that all the cars in a given class run the same number of laps between refueling stops, it should take the same amount of time to refuel those different cars so as not to offer a manufacturer or manufacturers an unfair advantage during pit stops.

So far so good but, as different makes of cars have different fuel tank capacities, a bit of juggling is required to ensure that cars not only have the same range on a single tank of fuel, but they take the same length of time to refuel. The FIA's solution? Regulate the flow of fuel. Simply put, cars with larger tanks (that otherwise take longer to fill than smaller capacity tanks) are afforded a higher fuel flow rate than cars with smaller tanks. But with the onboard fuel tank capacity subject to adjustment based on, among other things, BoP tweaks to weight, power and downforce, the exercise presents a moving target…especially when not all rules are written in black and white.

"They'd given us a capacity adjustment at the end of May

and we'd put the fuel delivery system together with the proper fuel regulator," O'Gara says. "We bought the restrictors from a recommended local fabricator, put them together and found we could do a fill in 28 seconds. Our partners on the WEC team said, 'That's no good.' I said, 'What do you mean? The fuel cell is the correct size, the restrictor is the correct size, the fuel hose is the correct length...' And they said 'Yeah, those are the rules but the FIA wants it to take 31 seconds to fuel the car.'

"There are four different rule books for Le Mans. I read them all backwards and forwards and there was nothing about 31 seconds in any of them," O'Gara continues. "But that's the stuff you can only learn by experiencing it. I went to Le Mans twice but never talked to teams in that kind of depth. We knew who to go to to fabricate the fuel restrictor, but nobody ever said anything about the 31 seconds."

Fortunately, the interchange between the IMSA and WEC teams was, if not entirely seamless, productive for both sides of the garage, although inevitably perhaps, the Indianapolis-based team benefitted most from the UK-based team's practical experience. In addition to alerting his counterparts to the 31-second "rule," for example, the WEC team's Steve "Jonah" Jones mentored the Indianapolis-based crew on the finer points of fueling procedures, while logistics boss Chuck Plummer helped organize the transfer of equipment from the shipping crates and the setup of the pit and garages.

"The car side, we had engineering meetings and technical bulletins coming out but then there's all the rest of the equipment side where there's nothing written down—it's all word of mouth," says O'Gara.

"A lot of it was just trial by fire, just doing things and figuring out what works and what doesn't work, what's allowed and what's not allowed. And the WEC guys, mechanics, engineers were great about us going over to their garage, watching and asking questions. 'I know you're doing your job but what am I supposed to do with this thing?' Or 'I've got this part and I don't even know what it is!'

"They were super cooperative...if we didn't have the WEC side it would have been so much more difficult than it was."

There was, of course, much more to Ford Chip Ganassi Racing's presence at Le Mans than the four garages full of Ford GTs and their associated crews. From the Ford and Ganassi suites

133

1966 Le Mans-winning Ford GT40 with proud owner Rob Kauffman (left) and friends.

above the team garages, Ford hospitality units in the paddock and overlooking the Ford Chicane to Ford Performance's "Ford Zone" (featuring Ford GT40 and Ford GTs constructed of Legos, not to mention a Circuit de la Sarthe replica slot car track complete with miniature Ford transporters), the Ford Performance souvenir shop and an abundance of advertising signs, the blue oval was—if not omnipresent—much in evidence at Le Mans.

On Wednesday morning virtually the entire Ford Chip Ganassi Racing contingent gathered at the Ford Zone to view an unabashedly emotional video featuring long-time Ford employees discussing their fierce loyalty to the company, followed by pep talks by Henry Ford III and Nair who, in their own ways, reminded the team they were representing not just the Ford brand but the extended Ford family—including everyone who has ever worked for Ford.

"You'll never race for that many people again. And unfortunately there's only once chance to celebrate a 50th anniversary," said Nair, before echoing the late Bruce McLaren's advice to Chris Amon in 1966 during the waning hours of the 24 Hours of Le Mans.

"All those people that bleed Ford blue, the only thing they're asking of us this weekend is to go like hell!"

In failing health, the 73-year-old Amon was unable to make the journey from New Zealand to join Ford, Nair and the rest of the Ford Chip Ganassi Racing team on the golden anniversary

Jay Ward reads Chris Amon's letter to the Ford team.

of his historic victory. However, his son was on hand and delivered a letter that Jay Ward, Director, Ford of Europe Product Communications, read to the assembled team.

Hi guys. First off, I'm very sorry that I'm unable to be there in person for this year's 24 Hours of Le Mans. But please note that I am with you there in spirit, and I will be following your progress with great interest. My son Alex will represent my family at the event but I wanted to send you all a personal note of good luck.

I think it's great that Ford is going back to Le Mans this year, and I'm sure you'll be very proud as I was that you've been called upon to take on this great challenge. I have very fond memories of 50 years ago. When I first started racing, the 24 Hours of Le Mans was—and still is—one of the most significant events on the international motorsport calendar. To have won that day back in 1966 and to have been part of Ford's first victory for me was personally huge. I was only 22 at the time and have to confess it took a few days for it all to sink in. The fact that so many still seem to remember our win I find gratifying, not only for myself but also for Bruce McLaren's memory for he, sadly, was only with us for too few years following our win in '66.

That said, I wish you all the very best for a safe and very successful race at Le Mans. Don't wait. Enjoy the moment. You'll be amazed at how quickly the next 50 years will pass.

135

Chapter 12
Practice and Qualifying

As THE FCGR CREWS CONTINUED preparing their cars, garages and pit boxes for the days and nights ahead, they still lacked a good read on how they stacked up against the competition. Sure they'd been a second to a second and a half off the pace of the fastest Corvette in pre-qualifying, but what did that mean? What shape were the Corvette's tires in when they set their quick times? New? Or did they have five, ten or more laps on them? What about the fuel load? Full, half or nearly empty tanks? Were the drivers running 10/10ths or 9/10ths? Or 8/10ths?

Heck, FCGR would have been hard pressed to say how fast its own cars were, let alone how they stacked up against the Aston Martins, Corvettes, Ferraris and Porsches.

"A lot of times people say, 'We were running full tanks and did this and this. If we did this and we did this and this, and add it all up…'" Hennek mused. "The same with aero calculations: 'If we put this bit on it's three pounds less drag; put that on it's five pounds less drag…' But when you add that all up, two plus two plus two doesn't equal six; it adds up to three or something.

"It was the same with us. 'If we took out all that weight from running full tanks that would be half a second. And let's run full rich, which will be more power so that should be another half second! Man we got this right where we want it.'

"Nobody was saying that on our side. And if they were, we weren't believing it. We really kind of didn't know where we stood."

In one respect, however, FCGR clearly had some catching up to do to their cross-town rivals.

Stopwatch in hand, Holt observed the Corvette crew practicing pit stops a couple of stalls away, gave the slightest shake of his head, and smiled.

"Clever," he said. "I gotta hand it to 'em. See how the right front goes up on the air jacks a little before the other three corners? The right front's the first tire they change, so it gives them a little edge."

A little edge for sure, but not enough to account for the fact the Corvette practice stops were, on average, a couple of seconds faster than those in the FCGR pits. Seventeen years of practice will do that...

Meanwhile, in the FCGR garages the team practiced the complex ballet of driver changes to O'Gara's stopwatch, with the two driving trios running through the procedure where the driver "on deck" opened the door, pulled back and secured the window netting as the driver in the cockpit undid his seat belts, attached the radio line from his helmet to a Velcro strip on the interior roof and clamored out of the car. A split second later, the process reversed itself with the "exited" driver securing the window netting as the new driver plugged in the radio and fastened his seat belts, with the exited driver firmly shutting the door just about the time the new driver clicked the last belt into place on the six-point harness...all in around 25 seconds.

There was plenty of time for driver swap practice, what with the on-track sessions not slated to begin until late Wednesday afternoon. And while there was another four hours of practice followed by two more hours of qualifying from 10 p.m. until midnight Thursday, all signs pointed to the grid being set Wednesday. The weather forecast indicated the fluctuating conditions that had visited the circuit since the weekend—dry and blustery one moment, rain showers the next, followed by bright sunshine—would be at their best on Wednesday evening. That was particularly the case for the Fords and Ferraris, whose turbocharged engines figured to function that little bit more efficiently in the low barometric pressure conditions predicted for the first night of qualifying.

"We expected Thursday to be wet, so Wednesday really was our day," Sole said.

But how best to take advantage of it? With enough vestiges of sunlight lingering to qualify as dusk at this latitude, did the teams go for a fast time in the opening minutes of qualifying when there was still a little natural light illuminating the circuit? Or did they wait until later when the marginally cooler temperatures—coupled with the rubber from hundreds of laps earlier in the session—made for peak "mechanical" conditions, albeit when the drivers had to rely on their headlights for illumination?

The WEC side opted to go fast early in the practice, with Pla and Tincknell setting the early pace at 3:55.081 and 3:55.436, respectively, although Bourdais was right behind at 3:55.928, ahead of Toni Vilander in the Risi Ferrari. Meanwhile the #69 Ford GT was "languishing" down the order with Dixon in the 3:59s. Still, given the fact that the IndyCar champion's sum total of seat time at Le Mans had come in the single day of prequalifying practice, all was going according to plan.

"What this program needs is for Scott to have the most time in the car," Goldberg explained. "The car's fast, Richard and Ryan are up to speed, I want a good race car. So we started on full tanks, second stint on the tires, put Dixon in and said: 'Don't come in until you run out of fuel.'"

Interrupted by a couple of rain showers, the practice session saw the AF Corse and Risi Ferraris come to the fore in the latter stages to top the time sheets at 3:53.833 and 3:54.180, respectively. Bourdais jumped to the top of the Ford contingent with a 3:54.893, ahead of Pla and Tincknell while Dixon worked

Pla set the early qualifying pace.

his way down to a 3:56.775.

The only disquieting news was that shortly after 7 p.m. Johnson spun on an "out lap" and slid into the tire wall, albeit lightly. Fortunately, the car suffered only superficial bodywork damage.

"I have no idea what happened," the American said. "The tires were up to temperature, up to pressure, but I wasn't pushing it. I braked way early and the next thing I knew I was doing a 360."

The car was easily repaired in time for the qualifying session when, once again, the WEC team's cars went fast early...make that very fast. Pla set a blistering pace at 3:52.038 with Tincknell not far behind at 3:52.553, sandwiching Gianmaria Bruni's AF Corse Ferrari at 3:52.090. Moments later Tincknell improved to a 3:51.590, only for Bruni to respond with a 3:51.568 before Giancarlo Fisichella spun the Risi Ferrari into the gravel trap in the Porsche Curves and out of the session. Moments later, Ricky Taylor gently nosed the #63 Corvette into the tire wall at Mulsanne Corner, although he reversed back onto the circuit and continued.

FCGR, it seemed, was not alone in believing the pole would be won or lost on Wednesday night.

Midway through the session the AF Corse Ferrari still held the top spot ahead of the two WEC Fords, the #71 Ferrari and the *hors de combat* Risi Ferrari. Although the IMSA Fords were several seconds off the pace, there was no sense of panic in their garages. Banking on conditions improving in the final hour, the #68 and #69 had spent the first half of the session working on race setups on used tires and full fuel loads, and the one time Hand had ventured out on fresh tires, he almost immediately encountered a red flag as the safety crews extracted Fisichella's "beached" Risi Ferrari from the gravel trap.

With half an hour remaining, the status quo held at the top of the time sheet...and further down as well where the Porsches, Aston Martins and Corvettes seemed unable to crack the 3:55 barrier. Although the IMSA Fords has also been off the pace, that was about to change.

"During safety car periods we worked on the car, made a few adjustments—little things like damper adjustments," said Goldberg. "There was about 30 minutes to go and it was 'OK that tire set is done, we're low on fuel...let's do something.'

"So we put on new tires and Ryan got in the car for his

qualifying run. He had a perfect lap until the safety zone came out and that was it for his new tire run. 'Oh crap,' I thought. 'We were on a good run, but that's OK: That's the nature of Le Mans.'

"We had already posted the fifth best time at the end of the second stint of tires, with Dixon in the car on full tanks, so I said 'We're probably not too bad.' So we brought Ryan in, made a change and because of the way the fueling operates we had to put half a fuel load in; then we sent him again for a second run on those tires."

This time there was no safety car, no yellow or red flags and no traffic. The result? 3:51.497. On half a load of fuel. On used tires.

"It was my second run on those tires and they had gone off," said Briscoe. "Still, it was a pretty good lap: clear, no traffic issues, but the last sector through the Porsche Curves was really 'sloppy.' I was thinking about pitting, but figured I might as well complete the lap. I crossed the line, saw 3:51.4 on the dash and thought 'Hey! That's the pole!'"

Not so fast. As Briscoe pitted to turn the car over to

Briscoe's 3:51.4—not bad for a 'sloppy' lap.

Westbrook, Müller was replacing Hand behind the wheel of the #68 Ford GT. He took to the track on fresh tires, a low fuel load and with pressure starting to mount. After all, stymied by traffic, yellows and the red flag, Hand had been unable to get out of the 3:55s.

"We decided to put on another set of tires at the end, hoping and anticipating rain for Thursday and saying, 'OK we can use this extra set of tires and we won't shoot ourselves in the foot for the race,'" said Hennek.

"Dirk went out and didn't seem to be going anywhere and I was starting to get concerned. Mike (O'Gara) was not concerned. He was saying, 'OK it's all about getting THE lap.' And it probably was true—not just for us but for everybody. It's such a long lap, and you have to be fortunate not to get any local yellows, you don't get traffic—there's so many things happening that unfortunately it's not down to car setup so much as it is getting the clear lap and can the driver do it on *the* lap."

"I didn't think it was going to happen. For two or three laps we kept getting guys in the Porsche Curves. You're looking and trying to tell him where traffic is, but it's impossible on an eight-mile track with people coming and going, to say, 'OK let's send him out here—there's a gap.' It really comes down to a bit of luck on getting the clear lap."

An out lap, a flying lap and traffic; a second flying lap, more traffic in the Porsche Curves. Then with ten minutes to go Müller got *the* lap: Every braking zone perfect, every apex nailed, no mistakes, no traffic and even a brief tow from an LMP1 car on the straight. The result? 3:51.185.

"I was a little under pressure," Müller said. "Joey kept getting his laps interrupted and we'd used one of set of tires for qualifying. Then I saw Ryan's time and I said, 'Oh my God. My teammate just got the pole.'

"The car felt good on the out lap and then I did a good flying lap but ran into traffic and did a 52.4. 'OK,' I said, 'be patient.' The next lap was good too, but I hit more traffic in the Porsche Curves and it was 51.7. The last lap there were cars in front, cars in back but I had a clear lap and I just got it. Really it was just coincidence that it was the last lap. I could have been quicker on the laps before but I ran into traffic…So now we do a rain dance for tomorrow night?!?!"

With Ford GTs first, second, fourth and fifth the FCGR garages were certainly in a celebratory mood. Perhaps not

Müller and Holt practice their rain dance.

dancing, but satisfied…for the time being.

"It was a good effort by everyone, drivers, mechanics, engineers," said Nair. "The cars responded to our qualifying setup perhaps better than we expected, but there were a lot of factors…yellows, changing conditions, the Ferrari and the Corvette went off the track. So we're not congratulating ourselves too much. But still, being first, second, fourth and fifth is better than not!"

"He had some pretty good laps before, but that time Dirk did the full lap without any interference and that's what did it," said Hennek. "At that point we thought that's all it had. And it was pretty good. Actually all of his laps were pretty good and the ACO looked at it and said, 'Oh, they are too good.'"

Indeed they did, but not until after another full day of preparations concluded—as predicted—with on again/off again rain for Thursday's practice and qualifying sessions in which nobody got within two seconds of Müller's pole-winning time. Still there was not much of a respite for the FCGR crews who, like most of their competitors, worked on rain settings, got their drivers more time on knobby tires and, in the process, accumulated more than 60 additional laps (in contrast to Aston Martin which never ventured out of their garages).

Ganassi, for one, was in a confident frame of mind, relaying a story of that afternoon's visit to the Americans at Le Mans exhibit in the public area of the paddock showcasing the Ford GTs that finished 1-2-3 at Le Mans in 1966 (including the Amon/McLaren car that had been meticulously restored by FCGR partner Rob Kauffman) along with one of Shelby's Cobra Daytona coupes and the Porsche 935 Paul Newman co-drove to second place in 1979.

"I asked the guy who organized the show, 'Are you going to have this exhibit here next year?' and he said, 'Certainly, Monsieur!'" Ganassi grinned. "I told him, 'You better plan on making it bigger.'"

"You know," he continued, quickly as serious as the proverbial heart attack, "we're gonna win this race unless the ACO does something stupid."

Having turned nearly 250 laps in prequalifying without breaking the 3:55 mark, the Ford GTs had indeed raised a lot of eyebrows in the paddock and in the ACO offices by lapping in

Ganassi suggested expansion plans for 2017.

the 3:51s in qualifying. The fastest Ferraris also knocked more than three seconds off their prequalifying times on Wednesday night but, in contrast, the Corvettes, Porsches and Aston Martins improved only marginally from pre-qualifying.

What was up? That depended on who you talked to and where their allegiances lay. The "s" word (sandbagging) was much in use around the paddock. But if teams were sandbagging, who was doing the sandbagging? And when? Had the Fords and Ferraris sandbagged in prequalifying, or were the Corvettes, Porsches and Aston Martins sandbagging now?

"The problem is not that we ran fast," said Pericak. "The problem is that the other guys didn't, and that's where we're most perplexed. There's no explanation for it. Ours is extremely explainable and we've explained it publically to all of the other manufacturers.

"When you go to qualify and you put barely enough fuel in to get around the track, and you put the best tires on, you pick up two seconds right there. That's just qualifying. Everybody should do that. So of the seconds that we improved, two of them are extremely explainable.

"(Wednesday) the barometric pressure was around 995, which gave a (turbo) boosted car an advantage," he continued. "Ferrari had the same advantage. Now at the end of the race we expect the pressure to be 1020 or higher, so we'll have a disadvantage. It goes both ways. But there's another explainable variant of about 1.3 seconds, so now we're at 3.3s of absolutely explainable difference.

"We had already declared coming in that we would be about a second faster. The FIA asked us: 'Based on our test day, when you come back, what do you think you'll show?' We said 'We believe by the time we get our car sorted out we're going to be able to improve by about a second.' We were very clear on that. So now we're at almost the entire explanation of why we ran what we ran. It's not perplexing why we ran what we ran; it's perplexing that the other guys did not."

Although the Ferraris had also gained more than four seconds over pre-qualifying, the view from the Risi Competizione pits was slightly different.

"Ferrari has been very straight with ACO—and IMSA—which hurts us because they approach it in the same way," said Rick Mayer, the team's race engineer. "But they've been very straight. They come around and ask us after the test, after the

Can we stop talking and go racing?

sessions 'How much fuel did you run? Did you run new tires? Did you run low fuel, new tires?' The ACO have all that data; they can figure it out, but Ferrari was very straightforward.

"Ford goes to Silverstone and they're what, two seconds off—that's pretty blatant. Then they go to Spa where the qualifying is the average of the two drivers' fastest laps and each driver does one timed lap and they park the cars? They're not trying. They're holding back. (Note: All of the GTE-Pro drivers did just one qualifying lap apiece at Spa.) And when you look at the timing data and you see the running averages and things, and the lines are very flat, that means they're running to a time.

"Obviously they ran the first four (IMSA) races and the first two races of WEC looking to bolster their chances at Le Mans. That's what they're doing. It's part of the game. It's what Corvette does and Porsche as well."

Doug Fehan, for one, would take issue with that last statement.

"One of the key elements in the BoP process is for the teams to demonstrate a car's capability all the time," he said. "And the sanctioning bodies both here and in the U.S. have asked us to do that. To the best of our ability we've complied; we run to the best of our ability virtually every time around there. And I think that's why when you saw our test day times and our qualifying times they were reasonably similar, although in qualifying we did have significantly less power due to the BoP adjustment.

"I can only speak to what we did. The pillars and tenets of what we operate on are honesty and integrity, respect and sportsmanship. We try and employ these at all times and that's what we've done. As far as what the others do, we keep our eye on what we're doing. We don't pay a lot of heed to what others are doing and they can choose their own operational methods and we rely on the sanctioning body to keep everybody even."

Holt was adamant the FCGR Ford GTs played it straight all along.

"Did we hide anything before last night?" he told *motorsport. com*'s Sam Smith on Thursday. "No, we never hid any performance per se. But we never went out to set a qualifying lap time.

"Where did the Ferrari time come from? They were three seconds quicker too. You do that in qualifying. That was an absolutely balls-out qualifying lap.

"I think there's probably over a second in the atmospheric table and a little bit [extra] just because we got carried away. I mean, Dirk [Müller] put one in right on the last lap. He got a tow, saw 301kph [on the Mulsanne straight].

"There is no way that the Corvette is that slow, no way," he continued. "They got a bad BoP break but there is no way that their pace is the pace they showed last night.

"The pace we showed last night, that's our pace. The pace Ferrari showed last night, that's their pace. Will we get some BoP [penalty] to even that out? Maybe we will."

Friday morning, the FIA removed any doubts when it released the following statement:

LM GTE Pro Balance of Performance change ahead of Le Mans

In line with article 7.4.3 of the Sporting Regulations and article 20 of the LM GTE Pro Technical Regulations, the FIA Endurance Committee has today revised the Balance of Performance (BoP) between LM GTE Pro-class cars ahead of the 24 Hours of Le Mans, the third round of the 2016 World Endurance Championship (WEC) season.

GT-class cars are originally production cars that can differ considerably from one another. A week-long series of tests was conducted last autumn to iron out these differences

and create a level playing field in terms of performance. The Endurance Committee has leeway to make further adjustments over the course of the season after examining the times set by each car.
Today's decision—which is final—concerns all five manufacturers competing in the LM GTE Pro class. In terms of weight, the Ferrari 488 GTE and the Ford GT must respectively take on board an extra 15 kg and 10 kg of ballast. The weight of the Porsche, Aston Martin and Chevrolet Corvette cars remains unchanged. Furthermore, the diameter of the air restrictor on the Vantage and the C7.R has been increased by 0.2 mm, resulting in increased power, while the Ford GT's turbo boost pressure has been reduced. Finally, fuel capacity has been increased by three litres on the Porsche 911 RSR (2016), and by two litres on the Ferrari and Corvette.
The decision takes effect from the 24 Hours of Le Mans which will start tomorrow, Saturday 18 June, at 15:00 local time.

Simply put, the FIA took measures intended to slow the Ford GTs and Ferrari 488GTEs incrementally while simultaneously slightly speeding-up the Aston Martin Vantages, Corvette C7.Rs and Porsche 911 RSRs. How much real world effect the BoP adjustments would have remained to be seen. Unmentioned in the statement was the fact that the upper limit on how "rich" the fuel/air mixture the Corvettes were permitted to run had been lowered by about 3 percent. Still, Fehan was encouraged, if guardedly, about the developments.

"We know, just from a common sense perspective, that an additional 2 mm of restrictor—that will be a couple of more horsepower, so that will certainly be beneficial," he said. "The question becomes on the turbos, where they're going to be, how far they're going to be dialed back. And only the race will tell that. It's impossible to really say.

"I don't think we'll be any quicker than we were on the test day. As the track rubbers up, it could—I'd be happy if we can run 3:55s and maybe if it gets good we can get into the 3:54s but I don't think there's much more than that…but time will tell."

The reaction in the FCGR garages was, if anything, even more muted. In reality, the BoP adjustments to the Ford GTs were hardly draconian. Ford engineers estimated the turbo

There are no quiet days at Le Mans.

boost adjustments would cost two or three horsepower, while the weight "penalty" probably did as much to help as hurt the cause. The Ford GTs were already over the minimum weight; what's more, they were on the verge of having too much of that weight on the rear of the car to satisfy the front/rear weight distribution homologated by the FIA. And the only easy means of getting down to the overall minimum weight would have been to remove some ballast from the fuel cell, which would have further tilted the weight balance to the rear. So adding the BoP-mandated 10kg to the front of the car enabled the Fords to get their front/rear weight distribution comfortably within the window homologated by the FIA.

And on a more philosophical level, Hull—for one—looked to turn the BoP adjustments to the team's advantage.

"What we do as a race team is we race the race and try to minimize the things that can stop us from being at the front at the end," he told *RACER*. "You win on racecraft, take what's given to you, and the faster you accept that, the faster you can push yourself to find the best strategy.

"What I like about what's happened with the [BoP change] is it's a compliment to what's Ford's done and the team's done and the sanctioning body's done. They try to make it fair. You have to accept what you're given. It's the most carnivorous class of racing. The race will demonstrate who has the best racecraft."

"This race is not going to be won or lost based on BoP," echoed Goldberg. "The outcome is going to be decided by reliability and who makes the fewest mistakes."

Pericak was even more succinct.

"Like I told everyone," he said, "'Can we just stop talking? Put the fuel in the car and let's go.'"

As matters turned out, that was easier said than done. A post-qualifying inspection on Thursday revealed a couple of potential "issues." First, some spherical bearings in the front uprights of all four Fords were showing signs of play. A call to a supplier in the north of England resulted in the overnight manufacture of replacements which were boxed-up, loaded into a car and driven to Le Mans where they were hand-delivered to Cadieux's hotel in the wee small hours of Satuday morning. They would be installed after sunrise that same morning in time for the pre-race warm up.

While that was in the works, the teams were also replacing the dog rings in the cars' gearboxes, this time owing to a manufacturing defect that resulted in potentially ruinous cracks. In the hopes of making for a relatively easy day on Friday, the WEC team had already invested time building its "race day" engine/transmission assemblies and running them in at the Monza test in anticipation of simply unbolting the engine/transmissions that had been used in practice and qualifying and replacing them with "fresh" ones. Not.

"We sent everybody home and took the back ends off the cars and wheeled them out down pit road on these trollies at 3 a.m.," says Cadieux. "Then wheeled the new engines back and had everything teed-up for Friday morning so when the crews came in fresh, it would be a relatively easy day for them. So all that work that you did, and all that frenzied pace you wanted to not have leading up to the race—Friday was supposed to be our 'quiet day' and we ended up being there to 3 a.m. the night before."

Chapter 13
UNSUNG HEROES

WHILE THE COUNTDOWN TO 3 P.M. on June 18 continued, Mel Harder was already up to his neck making plans for the people and hardware associated with Chip Ganassi Racing after 3:00:01 p.m. on June 19. As FCGR's recently appointed team manager, Harder had been in charge of the lion's share of the logistics associated with transporting a pair of race cars, some 10 tons of equipment and more than two dozen people from Indianapolis to Le Mans and back again as efficiently as possible.

But that's just for openers. Working with colleagues Shannon Logan and Suesan Potter, Harder coordinated travel itineraries for crew, drivers, managers, team executives and an assortment of VIPs and guests including the Mayo Clinic's Dr. Ian Hay, Indianapolis-based attorney Jim Voyles and his wife Joan, race driver-turned custom vehicle designer/collector Bruce Canepa, former Target executive Doug Scovanner and his wife Mary, Bruce Meyer, Founding Chairman of the Petersen Automotive Museum, Green High Performance Air Filters' Mark "Ford" German and Ralph DeSimone, Ganassi's mechanic when he began racing Formula Fords in the 1970s.

Harder also arranged for ground transportation in France including transfers to Le Mans from the airports in Paris and Angers, rental cars and vans, to say nothing of securing accommodations ranging from a couple of nights on race weekend to three-plus weeks for the crew...not to mention arranging for a private jet to fly Bourdais and Dixon from the IndyCar race at Texas Motor Speedway on the evening of June 11 in time for the public technical scrutineering session in the

Mel Harder

city center of Le Mans the following afternoon.

Harder was prepared for the job, having previously served as senior vice president of operations at the Indianapolis Motor Speedway and general manager of Circuit of the Americas in Texas. In both cases he was, in a sense, on the other end of equation as the point man—as it were—for Formula One teams coming to Indianapolis and Austin for the United States Grands Prix, not to mention the WEC race at CotA.

"From managing Fomula 1 and WEC races I was familiar with fly away races and the teams' expectations," says Harder, a trim man in his 40s with remarkably few gray hairs. "Really, apart from arranging the plane flights and hotel rooms it was pretty similar."

Perhaps most importantly, Harder knew what he didn't know. So he turned for advice to someone with over a decade of experience racing at Le Mans with an American-based team: Doug Fehan.

"What I gleaned from my conversation with Doug is that, being that far away for so long, it's important to take care of all the details," he says. "Traveling with 20-plus guys for 23 days, there's a lot of things that can happen, and the goal was making them as comfortable as possible. If you take care of the people the rest of the job will get done.

"I tried to have a plan with the maximum flexibility," he continues, "so it wasn't a case of: 'How am I ever going to make arrangements for this person or this one thing?' Everything had a pod to fit into, but I think that's what Chip was thinking, creating this position with Le Mans in mind to make sure the success was there. It was just another spoke in the wheel that made everything a little smoother."

In addition to Fehan, Harder relied on the WEC side of the team which also had a wealth of Le Mans experience and offered counsel on who, what and where to turn to get things done. While heeding his advisors, Harder also charted his own course from time-to-time, renting extra office space adjacent to their garages rather than following Corvette's practice of shipping their own, familiar transporter/office to the track. He also chose to house the crew in private homes in and around the circuit, affording them a better chance to unwind during the punishing sequence of long days (and nights) at the track rather than a typical hotel/restaurant scenario.

Too, the ACO itself was helpful, putting Harder in touch with an assortment of vendors who could be depended upon to deliver their services and goods ready and on time.

"Le Mans did a fantastic job of putting us together with vendors who you could count on to meet our expectations," he says, "anything from dry cleaning to the walls and the gantries we purchased. We had a massive purchase of items that were specific to this race: all the pit equipment was new, all the walls and the gantries were new, the awning out back, the flooring... all those things were new. So you had to count on them being there and being ready."

While the team sent one sea crate worth of equipment to Le Mans, with all the additional material they acquired in France for the race, they had three containers worth of stuff to deal with by the time the checkered flag waved on Sunday. Good thing the race was 24 hours long.

"It was nice that the race went so long because it gave me time to work on things," Harder laughs. "So it wasn't like I kicked back when the race started or in the middle of the night.

"Right up until the moment we left the track on Monday we were thrashing to get all the freight loaded. It was raining, the guys had just had a few hours of sleep after working something like 40 hours. We had to have all the freight loaded by 4 p.m. and, 'Oh by the way—we have a train at 5:30.'"

In the end, about half the team took the train to Paris while the rest drove or rode along to Orly Airport where they returned the rental cars, stayed in hotels for the night, then flew home Tuesday. Even then it wasn't over, as bad weather on the East Coast resulted in flight cancellations, requiring several team members to sleep in Dulles Airport and book flights back to Indianapolis on Wednesday.

"The logistics never stopped until we got home," said Harder.

Perhaps by the time the IMSA team got back to Indianapolis, Thierry Lecourt—the team's unofficial "Le Mans expert"—was allowing himself to relax. Official or not, Lecourt's title was appropriate and not just because he had competed at Le Mans as a team owner in the '90s and early 2000s, running a McLaren GT team and, later, working with DAMS Racing when they ran a Riley Engineering-designed Cadillac prototype. Through his friendship with Bob and Bill Riley, O'Gara met Lecourt during his reconnaissance trip to Le Mans in 2014. Lecourt was working as the Rileys' *de facto* liaison with the ACO at the time and O'Gara put dibs on his services should the Rileys not need him in 2016. When, rather than running his own program at Le Mans this year, Bill Riley opted to work with the Murphy LMP2 prototype, the door opened for Lecourt to work for FCGR.

"Bill said: 'You need to have somebody who knows this place, how to get around, and who knows who to talk to with the ACO,'" says O'Gara. "There's no way we would have gotten done what we did without Thierry.

"One of the first days there, I had to pick up some electronics from the ACO and Thierry said, 'I'll go with you, I'll show you where the offices are.' So we walk into the office and the officials are going, 'Hey Thierry! Great to see you!' I thought: 'We've got the right guy.'"

O'Gara would be proven right. Repeatedly. Such as on the Friday before pre-qualifying when Lecourt drove to a race shop in Belgium to collect a pair of seat belts with official FIA approval patches to replace the virtually identical seat belts the team had installed at Daytona, albeit without the FIA patches— or the associated licensing fees.

Then there was the time when, after replacing the fuel regulators, the IMSA and WEC teams needed to pump the fuel from their underground tanks into their pit rig tanks—a job reserved for an ACO official.

"The night before the test day it got to be 6 o'clock in the

Thierry Lecourt

evening and we still didn't have the fuel pump turned on to pump fuel into our rigs," O'Gara recalls. "The first guy the WEC team talked to said, 'Sorry Monsieur but we're done. It's 6 o'clock and we're going home.'

"So Thierry talked to a guy and it turned out he knew another guy who could do it who was just hanging around the track. He wasn't in his office, but Thierry found him and he was happy to turn on the pumps. We had fuel that night."

Harder and Lecourt are just two examples of scores of people whose efforts went largely unnoticed by the television crews, journalists and lifestyle reporters paying regular visits to the FCGR garages. Little did they know about the contributions made by the others like Victor Martinez, Peter Gibbons, Mark Thaxton and teams of people well-versed in virtual reality.

Martinez hasn't made it to Le Mans—yet. But that doesn't mean his fingerprints were not all over the Ford EcoBoost engine powering the Ford GTs. Recruited out of the University of Florida's School of Engineering for a Ford College Graduate (FCG) internship, Martinez was eventually hired full time in 2010 and placed in a 24-month rotation through every department in the Ford engine program before being assigned to the group developing future applications for four-cylinder turbocharged engines.

"During the course of the rotation you learn just enough about every aspect of engines to be dangerous," he laughs. "In reality, you get to know experienced, knowledgeable people throughout the engine program so any time you have a question about something, you know who to go to for answers."

A racer at heart, when Martinez learned of the EcoBoost engine project he put his name in the hat and, to his delight, was assigned to the Ford Performance group working on the 3.5-liter V6, initially working on the intake and exhaust systems. With the Daytona Prototype giving way to the Ford GT program he continued working on maximizing the efficiency of the air pathways, integrating the turbocharger with the intake and exhaust as well as working on the cam drive.

Although he was a regular presence during the FCGR test program over the fall and winter months of 2015/16, Martinez was nowhere to be found at Le Mans. While there is not a resentful bone in Martinez' body about being left-off Ford's "travelling squad," he does have one regret about Le Mans:

"My biggest wish?" he says. "I wish I would have paid out of my pocket to attend the race."

Victor Martinez with some of his handiwork.

Life After the Merry-go-Round

Throughout practice and qualifying at Le Mans, one man glided back and forth between the IMSA and WEC Ford Chip Ganassi Racing garages seemingly unnoticed, quietly assimilating the data on the computer monitors and, briefly, engaging in conversations with the race engineers before—just as unobtrusively—vanishing, only to reappear on the other side of the garage.

Little would the casual observer guess the FCGR go-between had been among the most highly respected race engineers in Indy car racing for more than three decades. Yet, with stints at Patrick Racing (where he worked with an up and coming race driver named Chip Ganassi), Penske Racing, Newman/Haas Racing and Andretti Motorsports, Peter Gibbons has no fewer than half a dozen IndyCar and four Indianapolis 500 championship rings.

Gibbons called it quits with Indy car racing and joined Multimatic as Technical Director of Vehicle Dynamics in 2010.

"I'd been involved with Larry (Holt) and Multimatic for almost a decade, so we've known each other for a long, long time," says Gibbons. "There were a lot of synergies and I was certainly 'over' IndyCar racing so I figured this was the time to get off the merry-go-round. So I did."

Gibbons' first projects included bringing Multimatic's DLI simulator online and working with the Lars Ogilvie-headed modeling group and what he calls "a really great group of vehicle dynamicists, some of the most talented I've ever worked with in my life. I've learned a lot and really had a lot of fun along the way.

"Multimatic is not just racing," he continues. "There's a lot of other programs including road cars. I'm involved with the Multimatic-Riley LMP2 program, sort of trying to merge the aero and mechanical. We do all of the aerodynamics modeling for Mazda, so we're intimately involved with that. There's always something new coming along. Larry Holt is amazing in that way. I'm not bored at all."

Speaking of something new, Gibbons has been involved with the Ford GT race and production cars from Day One, working on the aerodynamics with another former IndyCar (and Formula One colleague) Dr. Mark Handford on the cars' design and initial development and with young race engineer Steve Curtis once Multimatic began testing the Ford GT.

Once the IMSA team got their Ford GTs up and running,

Peter Gibbons

Gibbons largely focused on the Ford GT production car then helped the WEC ramp-up and also continued his simulation work. But the climax of his involvement with the Ford GT came at Le Mans, where he served as combination liaison and catalyst between the IMSA and WEC sides of the garage, particularly with Multimatic's embedded engineers.

"We had the advantage of working with four cars—that's four sets of information. You can think you have a lot of time but you don't have a lot of time," he says. "Multimatic have engineers placed within the teams: Jamie Leveille is a very talented young vehicle dynamicist—he's placed with Ganassi. Then there's Vince Libertucci who is placed with the WEC team and they've worked with Lars and I.

"We've been in the background helping and making sure there's cross-fertilization and ideas being passed back and forth. At Le Mans we took all four groups and everybody worked so well together; it was a lot of fun. It was a great group with a common goal—we didn't care who won, just as long as it was Ford GT."

The Magic Mountain

The rolling hills of Pennsylvania in the Northern United States hold a mysterious secret buried deep under Laurel Ridge. This highly classified test site is re-writing the textbooks on aerodynamic development.

So begins Sam Collins' article in *RaceCar Engineering* in the best-researched—if a trifle speculative (and somewhat geographically challenged)—account of one of motorsports' most intriguingly secretive facilities. Known variously as Chip Ganassi Racing's wind-less tunnel or Chip's Magic Mountain, the "highly classified test site" is located in the formerly abandoned Laurel Hill tunnel of the Pennsylvania Turnpike. Originally designed and partially excavated for a stillborn rail link between Pittsburgh and eastern Pennsylvania, the two-lane tunnel was completed and integrated into the Turnpike when it opened for business in 1940. After just 24 years of use, however, the tunnel was rendered obsolete by a four-lane bypass cutting through the top of Laurel Ridge.

The tunnel had been abandoned for nearly four decades when the Ganasi engineers suggested it would be beneficial if

Mark Paxton

the team had access to an abandoned drag strip to conduct full-scale aerodynamic testing. Better yet, if walls were built on each side of the strip, it would eliminate the swirling cross currents that are the bane of accurate data analysis in out of doors testing.

"When they said it would be ideal if we could build a roof over it, I said 'You mean like a tunnel?'" laughs the Pittsburgh born and bred Ganassi. "'I know where there's a tunnel.'"

After proof of concept tests confirmed the project's feasibility, Ganassi Racing leased and rehabilitated the near mile-long tunnel for its own purposes—creating a unique facility where full-scale aerodynamic, rolling resistance and other "useful" tests can be conducted in a rigidly controlled environment. Not only are there no crosswinds but, as anyone who has ever gone spelunking can attest, the ambient temperature inside the tunnel never varies more than a degree or two, winter, spring, summer or fall...unless someone wants it to!

Australian-born Mark Paxton manages the facility. He immigrated to the United States in the early-'90s and, after working as a race engineer for Willi Oppliger's Toyota Atlantic effort, joined Ganassi's team in late 1995. Working in support of renowned race engineer Morris Nunn, Paxton was part of an exhilarating ride that saw the team win four straight IndyCar titles with Jimmy Vasser, Alex Zanardi and Juan Pablo Montoya.

"The timing was unbelievable," he says. "It was the beginning of an era and I was there through the whole experience."

Paxton subsequently worked with Julian Robertson (now Ganassi Racing engineering team manager) on the IndyCars of Vasser, Bruno Junqueira and others before engineering the IndyCars of Jeff Ward and Scott Dixon in 2002, then moved to the R&D side with Ganassi's NASCAR program before assuming responsibility for managing the wind-less tunnel.

The affable Aussie chooses his words carefully, albeit politely, when discussing the tunnel which, by the way, utilizes a patented process (U.S. patent number 7,131,319 B2 to be precise) and which Ganassi prefers to term as a "private" rather a "secret" facility.

"I've been involved with the tunnel since Day One," Paxton says. "We did a proof of concept test in the Fall of 2003 and proved internally that the concept would work. There was a lot of work done later in 2003 including re-paving the tunnel, then we started using the facility in 2004. It's been a big part of our development process since then.

"I'm responsible for the facility itself, but our race teams are responsible for their own testing. However, I did attend the bulk of the testing they did in 2015 with the Ford GT because it's important to have continuity across the programs."

Although some of the tunnel's staff live near the facility, Paxton calls Indianapolis home and "super commutes" between the Hoosier and Keystone states. He is justifiably proud of the role the tunnel has played in Chip Ganassi Racing's many successes over the past dozen seasons—and the fact that facility truly does enable "top secret" testing, no matter how Ganassi parses his words.

Indeed, Paxton derives particular pleasure from the fact that one enterprising journalist spent several days poking around the area, asking local residents about the goings on at the "highly classified test site" and came up empty in terms of classified information.

"Over in Somerset, the closest town to Ganassi's tunnel" wrote *Road & Track*'s Larry Webster, "I found that almost everyone knew about it, but free talk was impossible to come by."

The Magic Mountain, it seems, knows how to keep its secrets.

Seeing is Believing

Impressive (some might say astonishing) as the quickening in the Ford GTs' pace between the pre-qualifying practice in early June and the race week qualifying session may have been, it could have been even more impressive/astonishing if only Ford Chip Ganassi Racing had believed the numbers produced by state-of-the-art racing simulators at Multimatic's Toronto facility and the Ford Performance Technical Center in Charlotte.

"We ran a lot on the simulators between the test and practice and qualifying of race week," Multimatic's Peter Gibbons says. "We continued to refine the setups and that proved quite beneficial."

"We spent a lot of time on the simulators between pre-qualifying and race week," Briscoe confirms. "We made some big gains in the setup: If we had completely trusted the data we'd have made even bigger gains."

Once upon a time, the ability of teams and manufacturers to test and develop race cars at race tracks, skid pads and private facilities was limited only by the weather and their operating budgets. In recent years however, in an effort to control ever escalating costs, virtually every major professional race sanctioning body has imposed limits on the amount of track testing by teams and manufacturers. In part because of these limits (and also due to breathtaking advances in the state-of-the-art), teams and manufacturers have increasingly turned to computerized simulation programs—often coupled with cockpit/pods simulating the visual, audio and physical (g-force) inputs drivers experience behind the wheel—to do their testing and development.

The advantages are legion: although state-of-the-art simulation soft- and hardware costs millions of dollars, that expense is partially offset by the reduced costs of transporting cars, support equipment and crew to the track, to say nothing of the costs associated with actually running the cars. While track testing is generally restricted to daylight hours and fair weather, simulators can run 24 hours a day, 365 days a year under precisely controlled conditions. Changes in chassis setups, aerodynamic settings and suspension geometry that can take half a day at the track are effected on the simulator with a few clicks of a computer mouse, and (so far at least) no driver has ever been injured, nor has a car been damaged, by a crash on the simulator.

But as Briscoe's comments suggest, the $64 question is how closely the simulation test data match real world results.

Multimatic DIL simulator

"We spend a lot of time correlating the base simulation model in our test labs—the kinematic appliance rig, the vehicle inertia facility, characterizing the tires, all of the components—shocks, brakes, everything," says Mark Rushbrook. "Then there's vehicle correlation work to make sure that, at the vehicle level, the simulation program is properly predicting what is going to happen on the track. Once we have confidence in that model, we can take it to the simulator and use that simulation model as the physics engine behind the simulator so that as the driver drives the simulator we've got good correlation with it."

Suffice to say, for Ford, Multimatic and other automotive companies, simulations have broader applications than "just" race cars

"Our simulation programs are working really well across all of our programs whether it's the Ford GT in racing or the Ford GT road car, for our NASCAR programs, also a lot our other Ford Performance car programs," says Rushbrook. "Even a lot of our mainstream car programs are using the same simulation and simulator tools to reduce development time and make the product even better.

"In racing, it's critical that when we show up at the track we know what we're going to unload with and, as the track conditions change, we know how sensitive all the different tuning 'knobs' are so that we know what to change on the car to adjust to different conditions.

"On the road car side, obviously, it's not as critical as getting to a race and being fast, but it is critical from the standpoint that prototypes are expensive. With the simulator you can do development work even before you have hard parts, hard cars—and making changes is a lot easier, a lot faster and a lot more affordable."

Correlating the simulation data on the cars and their various systems is only part of the process. As Rushbrook's partners Chip Ganassi and Michelin will attest, road car or race car, every aspect of every vehicle's performance is, ultimately, transmitted to the road through its tires. And understanding that meeting of rubber and road is every bit as important as knowing how much downforce/drag will be generated by lowering a car's ride height by 1/16".

"We scan all the tracks both for the graphics to feed the simulator then also for the surface itself to get the microtexture so we can fully characterize the tire/road interface, the contact patch," says Rushbrook. "One of the things that is difficult to get right is the friction level. A lot of times we'll take a friction tester to characterize the grip level of the track, the friction level, and to try to understand the way it changes from sun load and atmospheric conditions."

So when it comes to pinpointing the reason for the Ford GTs' remarkable performance gains at Le Mans between early and mid-June, by all means consider the usual suspects—low fuel, sticker tires, turbo-friendly atmospheric conditions, fiercely competitive drivers, Ford GT-friendly BoP and yes even sandbagging—but overlook the Multimatic and Ford simulation programs at your own peril.

Chapter 14
Race Day

THREE-HUNDRED AND NINETY-FOUR DAYS AFTER THE FORD GT turned its first lap at a relatively obscure race track in eastern Ontario, four Ford GTs lined up for the 2016 24 Hours of Le Mans in first, second, fourth and fifth on the GTE-Pro grid, separated from a sweep of the top four starting positions only by the AF Corse Ferrari. In their rear view mirrors was more than a year of testing, development, more testing, more development, countless hours in race shops from Indiana to Ontario to Oxfordshire, broken dog rings, failed shift activators, faulty door latches, a fire, a monstrous crash and more problematic dog rings. But also tremendous progress in speed and reliability, a victory at Mazda Raceway Laguna Seca Raceway, a runner-up finish at Circuit de Spa-Francorchamps and Wednesday night's electrifying qualifying performance.

The team and their suppliers had embodied the words of Henry Ford when he said: "Don't find fault, find remedies."

What lay ahead in the next 24 hours was anybody's guess. But to a man and woman in the FCGR garages, the hope was that nothing less than 24 hours of racing were just over the horizon, for any car that runs the full 24 hours stands a chance of winning.

"I always say winning races is almost impossible," said a philosophical Priaulx. "And I think going to Le Mans and winning Le Mans is almost impossible. But it is the same for everybody. Everybody has got the same challenges. I think we've got ourselves a 24-hour car now. I think we've got ourselves a top endurance team. The product is designed for Le Mans, so I can't see any reason why it's not possible. But you

Le Mans pit lane on race day: like no other place on Earth.

have to go into it like it's almost impossible; that's the approach you have to take in terms of what you need to do as a driver and what you need to do as a team—you've got to approach it like it's almost impossible and you've got to work to achieve the impossible."

As the oversized Rolex clocks above pit lane clicked ever closer to 3 p.m. and upwards of 100,000 men, women and children gathered in and around the grandstands and suites lining the pit straightaway sang *La Marseilles* (and Nair took a tumble scrambling over the pit wall from the grid) it became increasingly clear the race was in for a wet start. But how wet?

A torrential rain began pelting down about 2:45, sending those teams that had not already fitted rain tires on their cars scrambling to replace racing slicks with grooved rubber. But full rain tires or intermediates? The downpour soon gave way to a drizzle that, with brightening skies all 'round, seemed sure to abate shortly.

The #69 rolled out to the grid on slick tires, changed to intermediates and, just before the grid moved away for the formation lap, went to full rains. The #68 went to the grid on slicks but changed to intermediates with extra hand-cut grooves, while the #66 and #67 started (and stayed) on Michelin's standard intermediates.

Tire choice was the least of Priaulx's concerns. During the morning warmup the #67 Ford GT had experienced gear-shifting problems—possibly stemming from Friday's unscheduled gearbox rebuild. Although the crew thought they had fixed the issue, on the formation lap Priaulx reported he could not engage first and second gear properly. He pulled into the pits as the field completed the lap and the WEC crew went to work on the car.

"There was a pneumatic issue—we were losing pressure—and that was causing intermittent problems with the gear changes in the warmup," says Sole. "It came and went and by the time we got the car back in the pits, there were no issues. Obviously finding a problem that's gone away is much harder than finding it while you've still got it. We thought we'd found the source of the problem and fixed it...but it came back."

The track was so wet that ACO officials opted to start the race under full-course yellow and run the first few laps behind the pace car. Even with the field trundling around behind the pace car it was more than ten agonizing minutes before the problem on the #67 was traced and repaired. When Priaulx re-fired the Ford EcoBoost and drove down pit lane to rejoin the field, he was two laps down. Thus were Priaulx, Franchitti, Tinknell and their crew looking at racing for nearly 24 hours with almost no hope of winning. Barring what amounted to an act of God, even earning even a spot on the podium was, in a word, impossible.

"I was out on the grid and one minute I'm getting ready for the biggest race of the year and the next minute I'm being wheeled into the garage and I know it's over," said Priaulx. "And the hardest thing is you've got 23 hours and 59 minutes of driving at 11/10ths, risking your life for not a lot—just personal honor really. Yeah, it was tough; very tough."

The fans were less concerned about the ill fortune visited upon Priaulx than the fact the field continued circulating behind the pace car. They wanted to see a race and, as the increasingly vociferous cat calls and whistles emanating from the grandstands and spectator enclosures testified, by the sixth "race" lap behind the pace car, they were losing their patience.

However, the seventh time was the charm and all 60 starters charged past the waving green flag towards the first chicane and the Dunlop Bridge in a cloud of spray. Müller retained the GTE-Pro lead through the first lap but the #51 Ferrari muscled its way past Westbook as the #82 Ferrari moved into fourth ahead of Pla on the opening lap.

The Fords ran one-two at first.

With tens of thousands of gallons of water being evacuated by the 240 rain and intermediate tires, however, a dry line was already forming around most of the track by the end of the first lap. It was only matter of time before the cars stopped for slick tires. Priaulx and Westbrook were in for slicks at the end of the second flying lap, while Müller and Pla waited another round to stop—to their detriment.

For when all the cars cycled through their stops for slick tires, who but the #92 Porsche should be leading from Westbrook by a whopping 15 seconds, with Müller and Pla in tenth and eleventh in class, some 45 seconds adrift of first place.

"We screwed up on the first rain tire call," says Hennek. "The #69 guys came in after one lap, while Dirk was saying 'It still feels a little wet out here.' So we did the cautious thing: one more lap on rains rather than one lap too early on slicks and wad the thing up in the first hour.

"They came in, the track was dry and the next thing you know they were 15s or 20s ahead of us.

"But it's a long race and you can't worry about it. You just

167

say, 'Well we've given these guys 15 or 20 seconds. Am I ever gonna get that back?' In IMSA sometimes you get that back pretty easily but you don't get anything back easily at Le Mans. It might take your three hours to get 15 seconds back."

In the case of the #69 car, it took roughly ten laps to erase the 15-second deficit to the #92 Porsche, with Westbrook taking the class lead on Lap 22. Although the lead lasted only until Westbrook made his first fuel stop the following lap, when everyone cycled through their first round of scheduled stops Westbrook had regained the lead from #51, #82 and #71 Ferraris with Müller up to fifth, and now only 20s out of the lead.

Over the next hour and a half, Westbrook continued to lead from the #51 and #82 Ferraris by a few seconds while Müller ran in fourth, having disposed of the #71 Ferrari. The #82 Risi Ferrari was another matter, however, and closed on Westbrook's tail coming up to the second scheduled stops and, in fact, took the lead on the pit stop exchange as Westbrook handed over to Briscoe. Meanwhile, Müller had continued closing the gap and, soon after handing off to Hand, the #68 Ford GT moved around the #69 Ford to take up position on the tail of the Risi Ferrari. With the #66 in fourth spot about half a minute behind the leaders, Fords now ran 2-3-4…that is until Hand swept past the Risi Ferrari in the second chicane on the Mulsanne Straight on Lap 60, with Briscoe coming through three laps later.

Over the next hours Hand continued leading, drawing away from the #69—now with Dixon at the wheel—while Mücke and Matteo Malucelli in the Risi Ferrari swapped third place half a minute behind Hand.

Although the #69 had initially led the Ford charge, the #68 was increasingly emerging as the stronger of the two, in no small part because Westbroook, Briscoe and now Dixon were reporting a handling imbalance.

"By the end of the first stint, Richard was saying the car was really, really loose—moreso than he could ever remember it," says Goldberg. "We double stinted on dry tires, then we put Ryan in and each driver said it was very loose, very hard to drive. Our lap times were OK, they weren't nearly as good as the #68, but they were on par with the Ferrari and everybody else. What was interesting was when we put Richard back in he reported the car was significantly more loose than even at the end of his first stint.

"That threw a flag to us. We started looking at the data and realized the aero balance was moving forward at a pretty decent rate, which would explain some of the loose. It was pretty obvious something had happened. From there on out it was just a case of running laps and keeping things short. We were basically tripling the tires and doubling the drivers. Because the car was such a handful to drive, we wanted to give the guys the most rest we possibly could."

Only later, much later, would the crew discover the "something" that happened was the front anti-roll bar had broken, within the first 20 laps of the race. What's more, with the broken anti-roll bar, the front splitter slowly but surely ground away its leading edge, exacerbating the imbalance.

In fourth place, meanwhile, Johnson, Mücke and Pla were matching the pace of the leader even as the #67 Ford GT continued in something of a guinea pig role: effectively out of the mix for a strong finish, the team could try setup and tire tactics and see if they worked with nothing much to lose if they didn't produce better performance—and everything to gain by applying the same tweaks to the other cars if they did.

Getting on towards dark, Hand's times began creeping up from the 3:54 range to the 3:56s as his Michelins approached,

Ford GT #67: 23:59 as a guinea pig.

reached and exceeded the end of their useful lifespan. Although he managed to retain the lead before handing-off to Bourdais, the Californian was in no rush to triple-stint his tires again.

"You could pretty much see the air in the tires when Joey came in," said O'Gara. "He said he was fine with triple-stinting the tires later in the race...as long as he wasn't driving."

In the hands of Bourdais the #68 continued leading from the Risi Ferrari and the #66 and #69 Ford GTs with all the other competitors a lap or more in arrears as darkness fell.

The second chink in the Ford armor occurred shortly after nightfall when the number panel lights failed on the side of the #66 Ford GT. ACO officials notified the team that their car would be black flagged and penalized if they did not fix the issue at the first opportunity, so the crew attended to the faulty lights on the next regularly scheduled stop.

The car's original design had the number panels integrated into the doors. But when it was determined that arrangement upset the cars' graphic "aesthetics," the panels were relocated to the rear quarter panel. Thus what had been a simple wiring scheme turned into a complicated exercise in electrical engineering requiring some eight feet of fly lead wiring snaking around the car's innards. Sure enough, some of the connections had gotten damp and failed—no doubt thanks to the race's rainy start. What's more, rather than swapping new doors for old doors (the work of a moment or two), the crew had to locate and replace the faulty connections. By the time #66 returned to action, more than a lap had been lost to the lead cars. Later, the same issue would afflict the star-crossed the #67 Ford GT.

The next chink in the armor reared its ugly head when, through a combination of bad luck (exacerbated by their unfamiliarity with the safety zone and safety car procedures), both the IMSA cars lost time doing their routine brake pad changes approaching the mid-point of the race.

First, with the brake change planned for the subsequent pit stop, Müller brought #68 to the pits for fuel and tires during a safety car period. When the servicing was complete, he motored to the end of pit lane and was held until the next safety car pack came around rather than being released to join his original pack. Then, figuring they could do the pad change the next time around under the safety car, the team called Müller in and fell behind to another safety pack.

"We spotted the Ferrari a minute or so with that brake

The #69 Ford GT never recovered from an ill-timed brake pad change.

change," said Hennek, "then spent the rest of the night trying to catch-up to them."

The #69 car also got bit by the safety car on its pad change. A safety zone was declared on the Mulsanne Straightaway, instantly turning the fastest section of the race track into an 80 kph zone, adding perhaps 30s to the lap times. When better to make an extended stop to replace the brake pads?

Except that, unknown to the FCGR crew, the safety zone was triggered by a car that stopped a few yards shy of a break in the Armco safety barrier. As Briscoe was entering pit lane, the efficient marshals were pushing the stricken car behind the barriers and the safety zone was removed before the Ford GT even reached its pit stall.

"That hurt," said Goldberg. "It detached us from the #68 and the Risi Ferrari and put a gap in between us. We would claw that gap back but we could never get close enough to them to get in the same slow zone cycle; sometimes there would be slow zones they missed and we didn't. So we would claw back some time and then lose it."

A similar scenario would unfold for the #68 Ford GT in the coming hours, but for entirely different reasons...and with an entirely different outcome.

Chapter 15
One in a Million

WHEN SEBASTIEN BOURDAIS took over the #68 Ford GT from Joey Hand shortly after 5 a.m., the car was a little more than a minute behind the leading Risi Ferrari. However, if anyone at FCGR could bring that gap down it was Bourdais, a formidable race driver under any circumstances but in this case one competing on his "home" circuit for the 11th time and who could probably lap la Sarthe in the pitch dark faster than most of his competitors in broad daylight.

What Bourdais couldn't know was that he was setting off on one of the wildest rides of his career. All went well initially, but it wasn't long into the stint before all radio communications with the FCGR pits vanished. While losing radio communications is a major inconvenience, race drivers operated quite well for three-quarters of a century without the benefit of two-way radios thanks to the fact that you don't miss what you never had in the first place. Also, their crews could impart vital information to them like lap times, the number of laps remaining and when to pit for fuel on "pit boards" (as simple as chalk on a blackboard, or as sophisticated as electronic pads with LED displays) they hung over the pit wall as the driver sped past each lap.

Although pit board "technology" went out with bias-ply tires and carburetors, every team carries pit boards to races in case of just such an eventuality as had befallen the #68 Ford GT. So once it became clear there had been a communications breakdown, the FCGR crew began signaling to Bourdais on their pit board.

But Bourdais couldn't read it in the glare of the headlights.

"It felt like the longest stint in my life," he said. "Basically you're on your own—no slow zone, no safety car advice and then you've got to pit on your own (without any coaching from the crew)...deciding when that was going to be appropriate, trying not to run out of gas but trying not to lose a lap either because if you stopped too soon you would have to make an extra pit stop at the end of the race."

Fortunately, the steering wheel's electronic data display was functioning, including a lap-by-lap fuel countdown of the number of laps before Bourdais had to pit. All well and good, but could the onboard computer be trusted? Much better to have a radio link to O'Gara and Hennek confirming the fuel countdown.

Bourdais trusted the countdown and it was right on the money. He made a routine fuel stop and returned to the track. What's more, Ken Brooks tracked down the source of the radio glitch (it was in the garage apparatus not the car) and soon effected repairs.

"The second stint we got the radio back," said Bourdais. "'OK,' I thought. 'It's back under control. Everything is good.'"

Good indeed. For all the communication problems, Bourdais had "clawed" his way back to within seven seconds of the Risi Ferrari when the second chapter of his crazy ride commenced.

"We triple-stinted the tires, which was tough because the performance was degrading quite a bit," Bourdais said. "But it was good because we had a safety car period, so we could follow the safety car around without putting too much stress on the tires...and then the steering wheel (electronics) froze. I couldn't see data, only the radio was working, and when I went into the pits the pit lane speed limiter wasn't working. So I was trying to gauge my speed from the Aston Martin ahead of me and not get a penalty for speeding in pit lane.

"Then when I came to a stop in the pit, I hit the kill switch on the steering wheel and the engine went brrrrrrrr...and then it started again."

The trouble was, the moment the engine shut-off, fueler Lee Blackwell plugged-in the fueling hose only for the engine to refire instantly incurring a penalty for refueling the car with the engine running, regardless of the extenuating circumstances.

"When I heard that engine start up again, my stomach sank," said Blackwell. "But what could I do but keep fueling the car? The only other option was to unplug the fuel hose, say 'Sorry,' and then plug-in again. I doubt the ACO would have bought it."

As Bourdais was reaching for the master switch on the

dashboard to cut all the electrical power, Müller had the door open, the window netting down and was trying to yank his teammate out of the car...which didn't work so well given the driver hadn't yet released his seat belts.

Meanwhile, Weaver had located a spare steering wheel and handed it off to Rees who, in turn, gave it to Bourdais. The beleaguered Frenchman pulled the quick release on the inert steering wheel, replaced it with the spare and finally, exited the car.

It was, in Bourdais' words, "quite special."

Fueling complete, Bourdais out, Müller belted-in, new steering wheel installed and four fresh Michelins swapped for the old ones, the #68 burbled to life. Müller engaged first gear and headed down pit road, destined to return a few laps later to serve a drive-through penalty for refueling with the engine running.

What had been a seven-second deficit had ballooned to 39 seconds. Unfazed, or perhaps energized, Müller set about reeling in the Ferrari driving—in the immortal words of Jake and Elwood Blue—"like he was on a mission from God."

Lapping a second, sometimes two, faster than Malucelli in the Risi Ferrari, Müller hauled the #68 back into striking distance of the lead over the next 40 laps. By the time he pulled into the pits to hand the car over the Hand, the gap stood at 3.2

seconds. Exiting the car, he accepted high fives from the crew before walking into the back of the garage for a cool drink.

"Unfortunately, Sebastien couldn't stop the engine," Müller said. "Yes, I had my head down a little when we got the drive-through penalty, but I knew it was possible to make up the time so I decided to go like hell. When I see that trophy ahead of me, I want to win!"

Moments later, Müller encountered Blackwell, who embraced him saying, "Great job, sorry I put you in a hole."

"Don't worry," said Müller. "It was not your fault; it couldn't be helped."

"We win as a team and we lose as a team," Blackwell said later. "Nobody said anything to me after the pit stop; they didn't have to. We're all leaving everything we've got on the table and everybody here has my back; just like I have theirs."

Still, there was a race to be won and Hand intended to win it. By the time he rejoined the action the gap to the Risi Ferrari—now in the hands of Toni Vilander—stood at 6.7 seconds. Four laps later it was down to 3.2 seconds. At the end of the next lap Hand crossed the line 1.8 seconds behind the Ferrari, then feinted to the inside approaching the chicane before the Dunlop Bridge. Two miles later on the Mulsanne Straight he pulled alongside the Ferrari, hesitated for an instant then swept past into the first chicane.

"We were on new tires and I wanted to take advantage of them," Hand said, "not only to get the lead but so that I could get out in front of him right away and get in clear air so it would be easy on the tires for the rest of my stint.

"I kind of baited him into Turn One, backed-off and then got a huge run out of Tertre Rouge," he explained. "Both cars were pretty similar in top speed: it was a matter of who got the draft. So I got up alongside of him and used a trick I've learned from my NASCAR buddies: When I got my front tire even with his rear tire I hesitated. That packs up the air in his wheel well—it's like opening a parachute on his car; probably cost him 3-4 mph. After I got around him I drove really hard for a lap or two to put some distance between us."

Not surprisingly, the FCGR garage area erupted in applause when Hand commandeered the lead. But as one veteran observer noted, it was not quite time to break out the champagne.

"I was sitting with Bill Ford and Joe Hinrichs (Ford Executive Vice President and President of the Americas) when Joey made

With new tires and a 40 second lead Müller heads to the finish.

the pass," Ganassi said. "Joe turned and said to me, 'That's great! What happens between now and 3 o'clock?' I said, 'A million things can happen...but only one of 'em's good.'"

According to his plan, Hand stretched his advantage to 2.5 seconds before the two leaders pitted on Lap 280. The gap continued to grow after the Ford and Ferrari returned to the track, up to 6.6 seconds by Lap 284...and then it began coming down: From 5.7 seconds on lap 286, to 3.8 seconds on Lap 288, to 2.9 seconds on Lap 289 and the next lap...Vilander spun exiting the Karting Esses. It was a tight spin—the Ferrari pirouetting over the curbing, stopping and quickly rejoining, suffering no damage other than to its now rectangular Michelins. But it gave Hand the breathing room he needed.

"I kept hitting traffic," said Hand, "and I could tell he was coming hard. He was using up the car, braking later and later. Then when he spun I thought: 'OK, that's what we needed.'"

In more ways than one. Vilander immediately made for the pits for fresh tires and a load of fuel, with Hand pitting two laps later. In addition to taking on fuel and swapping Hand for Müller, thanks to Vilander's spin, the crew now had time to slap on a fresh set of Michelins for the final run to the flag.

"When Joey got around those guys we didn't leave them; they weren't out of it at all," says Hennek. "But when Vilander spun, that was the big relief because changing tires during the next stop would have been a 20-second swing. If they don't change tires on that stop, maybe they get out in front of us and we've got to pass them again."

As it was, Müller took over with a nice time cushion, fresh tires and a Ford GT ready to go the rest of the distance.

"I wanted to give Dirk a clean race car," said Hand. "With two hours to go and a 40-second lead, the car didn't have a scratch and it was on new tires. It was like giving candy to a kid."

Indeed, on the track it merely remained for Müller to run a mistake-free final two hours to the checkered flag; by no means an easy task, but well within the comfort zone of a consummate professional.

"The last stint was so emotional, so many pictures were going in my head," Müller said. "I had to say: 'Hey! Focus. Focus. Don't do anything stupid. Just bring the car home.'"

That wasn't the only drama unfolding in the FCGR pits. Having clawed their own way back into a position where they had an outside shot at grabbing second place, the crew on the #69 car was debating a strategy move of their own. Some 25 seconds back of the Risi Ferrari and with one stop remaining, did they roll the dice and triple-stint their tires in an effort to close within striking distance of second place?

For despite the handling imbalance the car had exhibited since the second hour of the race, the #69 was still plenty fast. How fast? Consider that Dixon set what would be the fastest GTE-Pro lap of the race on Lap 329 (3:51.514)—nipping Johnson and the #66 Ford GT for that distinction by 0.068s—while doing his best to catch the Ferrari.

The trouble is he had taken a lot out of the tires to close the gap. In the end, Goldberg decided changing tires was not only prudent, it ultimately gave Dixon the best chance of catching and passing the Risi Ferrari.

"We absolutely wanted to triple-stint and I think that would have put us right with the Ferrari," Goldberg explained. "The problem is that we had to run very hard to catch him and with five or six laps to go to the stop we started losing time to the Ferrari.

"I told Scott we were thinking of doing a triple-stint and he

Risk vs Reward brought #69 home third.

said, 'Man these tires are going away pretty quickly.'

"Triple-stinting would have put us close, but it would have cost us so much time with the (continued) fall-off of performance, I'm pretty confident we'd have finished even further behind. We weren't that far back, and if the Ferrari had some sort of problem we'd have been able to attack him better on new tires.

"Also I didn't want to relinquish what we had already accomplished. That's the risk versus the reward. The risks are you might have to come in later to put new tires on, or get a puncture or have a blow out or if the car got away from the driver and then it's game over. That's the last thing we needed."

In the end, the status quo was maintained over the final two hours. Müller enjoyed a lead of 60.1 seconds when he got behind the wheel of the #68 for the final time, while the Risi Ferrari was up by half a minute on the #69 Ford GT. The #66 Ford GT was a lap down to the leaders, the fact that it trailed the #68 Ford GT by less time than had been required to repair its leader light panel a little more than 12 hours ago of small solace.

"We'll never know how close it would have been if we hadn't had the number light problem," said Mücke. "But to win

Le Mans you can't have any problems like that. All we could do was never give up, keep pushing, pushing and go as fast you can. That's all we could do. Yes the 68 and 69 were a lap ahead of us, but you never know what will happen to them and we had to be there to back them up if needed."

Fortunately, no backup was needed. As 3 p.m. approached, Müller was slightly more than a minute ahead of the Ferrari at the start of what would become a dramatic final lap. On the high-speed run from Mulsanne Corner to Indianapolis and Arnage, he passed a stupefied Neel Jani at wheel of the LMP1 Porsche that had inherited the overall win when the leading Toyota suffered a mechanical failure less than ten minutes from the finish.

The Toyota's demise triggered a veritable tsunami of emotions on pit lane, and not just in the Porsche and Toyota Gazoo Racing garages.

"With about a half hour to go, we were all getting excited; we could feel the energy growing and we were getting close and closer and closer," said Henry Ford III. "And then the lead Toyota collapsed. I thought to myself: 'Oh my God. What if that happens to us?' At that moment I started to panic a little bit on the inside and yet, at the same time, I just had a feeling that we were going to do it."

Indeed they were. Spurred by the ever-alert Bourdais, O'Gara radioed Müller to slow and allow the lead Porsche to repass, thus eliminating the need for the Ford to run an extra lap. Moments later a jubilant Müller took the checkered flag, precisely 395 days after the Ford GT first turned a wheel at Calabogie.

"When I passed the line all the emotions came out...but not really," Müller said. "I think it will take a few days to completely understand all we achieved today; what we achieved as a group with a whole team behind it. Chip Ganassi Racing, Ford, Multimatic—we are one team and it feels like we have done it already so many times and yet we are here for the first time. Can you get that? It's really amazing."

Not lost on anyone with a sense of history—particularly one named Edsel B. Ford II—was the fact the win came 50 years to the day after Amon and McLaren won the 1966 24 Hours of Le Mans.

"I was here 50 years ago today with my father and saw the same thing happen that happened today," Edsel said. "It's just absolutely unbelievable. I think the stars aligned. Once again we had to beat Ferrari. It was all about hard work and dedication

Exactly 50 years after their 1966 triumph, Ford claimed another checkered flag at Le Mans.

and people who really care. It's a very emotional moment for all of us."

Few would argue anybody worked harder, showed more dedication or cared more than Raj Nair.

"We did it for our employees, our families and everybody who loves Ford," said Nair to a soundtrack of cheers, back slaps, high fives and popping champagne corks in the bedlam of the FCGR garage. "I hope they're proud of us."

Bill Ford, for one, was certainly plenty proud.

"From the beginning we knew it had to be a partnership to get there, but building that partnership—Chip Ganassi Racing, Multimatic, Ford, Roush Yates Engines, Michelin, Brembo Brakes—everybody contributed to this in a very positive way to this happening today," he said. "The other thing that's amazing is that it was a very long trip here but in some ways it was a very quick trip. Boom! Here we are racing. And Boom! Here we are at the finish. It's incredible that we're here."

The Fords' presence certainly made an impression on

Sebastien Bourdais, even beyond winning his "home" race.

"As soon as the Ford family arrived, you could grasp the passion and the excitement and the reason why they were here and what it meant to them. It just gives such a different spin and another dimension to the whole program. It was unique… feeling so privileged and honored to be involved in it. That's what I'll remember the most. I've been part of some cool things, but to realize what and who you're racing for and what you're racing with, it just really separates it from everything that came before.

"It's so much greater than you, me and the team—it's symbolic of the whole scenario: the battle with Ferrari—the guy who wrote the script has got to be freakin' nuts. I mean how could it be more historically anecdotic, other than this. It's just insane. At the end of the day, the result is fitting; everything falls into place and I don't know…I'm kind of at a loss for words."

But not for actions. For there was one more Boom! left for Bill Ford, who made the mistake of standing next to Bourdais on the victory rostrum. Warning: Never get too close to a jubilant Frenchman with a loaded bottle of champagne in his hands; especially one who's sprayed a bottle of bubbly or two during his career.

Bedlam reigns in the FCGR garages.

A champagne toast 50 years in the making.

After priming the bottle with a light tap on the floor, Bourdais gave Ford—and his sinuses—a blast of champagne to remember. Later, Bourdais only half-jokingly wondered if his podium antics had jeopardized his chances of defending the GTE-Pro win with FCGR in 2017.

He needn't have worried.

"I've never enjoyed anything so much," said Ford. "The fact that I was blinded? Oh well, it was for a good cause."

Chapter 16
Epilogue I

As Dirk Müller, Scott Dixon, Olivier Pla and Andy Priaulx piloted their Ford GTs towards a finish only the most wild-eyed optimist at Ford, Ganassi or Multimatic could have imagined, a different kind of drama was unfolding in the Ford Chip Ganassi Racing and Risi Competizione garages.

For some time FCGR had been aware the position lights (three almond-shaped orbs that signal a top-three car's position in its class) on the second-placed Risi Ferrari had ceased operating. Earlier, the failures of the #66 and #67 Ford GTs' number panel lights came under the purview of the 2016 FIA World Endurance Championship Sporting Regulation 7.8 "Lights" which states: "in case of malfunction of a car's lighting and light signalling system, whether on the track or in the pit lane, the Race Director shall immediately inform the competitor, who must remedy the situation during the next pit stop, unless the Race Director, for safety reasons at his own discretion, decides to order the immediate stopping of the car in order for repairs to be carried out."

The failure of the Ferrari's positional lights fell under the Sporting Regulations' "systems and equipment imposed by the regulations and bulletins" paragraph 7.5.5, which states: "it is the responsibility of each competitor to obtain the systems or equipment from the Championship Promoter, to install them and to make them work correctly. If a system or equipment imposed by the regulations and bulletins fails to work" during a race the sanctions are as follows: "1st failure noted: Stop and Go until return to normal, 2nd failure noted: Stop and Go until return to normal + 2 minutes, 3rd failure noted: at the Stewards' discretion (exclusion possible)."

Unlike the Ganassi squad, the Risi team had not effected repairs on their car despite the fact that they had been notified of the issue and had had the opportunity to fix the lights on a pit stop.

When FCGR inquired about any pending action regarding the Ferrari, ACO officials informed them no action would be taken unless FCGR filed an official protest; that the ACO would penalize the Risi Ferrari if Ford protested but they would prefer they didn't protest.

After some consultation among the FCGR braintrust, Holt was deputized to pay a call on his friend, rival (and sometime Multimatic customer) Giuseppe Risi to explain the situation from FCGR's perspective: to tell him what the ACO had told FCGR, explain they did not want to protest and suggest the best course of action for all concerned would be for Risi to fix their lights.

According to Holt, Risi agreed and they parted company. However, when the Ferrari made another stop and—again—did not repair its positional lights, Nair began putting the wheels of filing a protest in motion.

"I told him to give me one more chance to ask Giuseppe why they hadn't fixed their lights," said Holt. "At that point it was about 1:50 p.m. and Raj told me: 'OK, you've got until 2 o'clock.'

"So I went down to the Risi office and, this time there were a lot of people there along with my friend Giuseppe; it was like I had walked into a Ferrari board meeting. It became evident to me that they weren't going to fix their lights. I said 'Fuck it!' and went back to our garage."

Ford subsequently filed an official protest and the ACO duly showed the #82 Ferrari the black and orange flag as the clock ticked towards 3 p.m.

When word of the protest circulated, so did righteous indignation among a variety of observers including Radio Le Mans' commentator John Hindhaugh. "That is an absolute travesty—at this stage of the race," he said. "It might be the letter of the law but people drove around for hours last night including Porsche, for hours at the start of the race, showing the wrong leader lights. We're inside the last 25 minutes and they're going to deny Fisichella and Risi Competizione a second

The podium celebration belied the drama unfolding in the stewards' office.

place on the podium and give Ford a potential 1-2-3. That is a travesty. Stay out and argue about it later guys. Do not answer that flag. That is ridiculous, absolutely ridiculous and puts the tin hat on the GTE fiasco that we have had over the last ten days or a fortnight."

Conveniently disregarded in the emotion of the moment was the fact that both WEC Fords had complied with the ACO's instructions to effect lighting repairs, to the detriment of the #66 in particular, which was as quick as the Risi Ferrari and the IMSA team's cars but never regained the time lost. Nor, evidently, were the indignant ones familiar with the grievance of sports fans the world over who regularly complain when officials "put their whistles away" in the waning moments of soccer, hockey, football and other stick 'n ball games.

Some cynics went so far as to suggest Ford and the ACO were conspiring to manage a fairy tale Ford 1-2-3 finish to match the 1966 results. However, events were about to transpire that made it abundantly clear that, even with a lead of over a minute in the final hour of the race, there were no guarantees Ford would finish 1-3-4, let alone 1-2-3. For even as an emotional Müller negotiated the final laps that stood between the #68 Ford GT and 3 p.m., one of the most emotionally charged finishes in the history of the 24 Hours of Le Mans was unfolding.

With over a minute's lead in the LMP1 class, Toyota was on the verge of defeating the powerful Audi and Porsche teams and earning its first overall win at Le Mans; a particularly rewarding achievement given the Japanese manufacturer had three times previously finished runner-up at Le Mans.

But with less than 10 minutes to go, driver Kazuki Nakajima frantically radioed that his Toyota TS050—Hybrid had lost power. Sure enough, Nakajima slowed midway through the lap and crawled to a stop in front of the Toyota pit as what had been the second-place Porsche swept past to lead the final lap. And in a particularly cruel twist of fate, although Nakajima eventually managed to coax the Toyota around for one more lap, because he failed to complete that final lap within the required time span—and thus was technically not running at the finish of the 24 hours—his Toyota was not even classified as a finisher.

On that painfully slow lap Nakajima was, of course, passed first by a jubilant Müller and about a minute later, by the Risi Ferrari, its positional lights still inoperative.

Perhaps those so quick to castigate Ford, Ganassi and Holt for their appalling lack of sportsmanship might have stopped to consider what would have happened had the #68 suffered a crippling mechanical problem akin to that experienced by the Toyota in the final hour? Or had Müller's concentration lapsed and he slid off the track? Or had a slower driver misjudged matters as Müller put another lap on him? Or had a faster LMP1 or LMP2 driver made a similar mistake while lapping Müller?

How would the ACO have reacted had Ford waited until *after* the race to protest the Ferrari that crossed the finish line first? How would Nair, Ganassi and Holt have explained to their constituents—including the crews who had given up weekends and holidays without number and worked countless hours into the nights—that they did not do everything in their power to win the 24 Hours of Le Mans; that their failure to protest the Ferrari during the race for a clear violation of the rules had, in all probability, cost them a victory?

Nobody can say of course. What can be said is that while Bourdais, Hand and Müller, Briscoe, Dixon and Westbrook celebrated their 1-3 finish on the podium (having been told by one irate official that their trophies would be confiscated following the victory ceremony) the ACO was hearing protests and counter-protests from FCGR and Risi. The former was reiterating its challenge to the fact the Ferrari completed the final hours of the race with its positional lights inoperable; the latter contended that, during his rousing comeback from the drive-through penalty, Müller had exceeded the speed limit through a safety zone—a claim supported by in-car camera video footage.

In the end the ACO levied a 50-second penalty on the #68 Ford GT (plus another 20 seconds for a faulty wheel speed sensor) and a 20-second penalty (plus 5000 Euros) on the #82 Ferrari—the net effect of which reduced the Ford GT's margin of victory from 60.2 to 10.2 seconds but left the finishing order unchanged.

And as a final postscript, in the wake of the controversy over the BoP regulations at Le Mans, the FIA posted the following statement on its website on July 19:

The FIA Endurance Committee last week issued a revised Balance of Performance (BoP) for LMGTE cars in the FIA World Endurance Championship, with Porsche and Aston Martin both likely to profit from the adjustments.

The LMGTE Pro Porsche 911 RSR gets a 15kg weight break (now 1233kg), and a 0.2mm increase in the size of its air restrictor ahead of the 6 Hours of Nürburgring, taking place this weekend (24 July).
The Aston Martin Vantage V8 GTE will have –20kg plus a 0.4mm larger air restrictor, as it used at Spa, and must use its Aero Kit 'C' which is a homologated high downforce aero package.
No changes have been made to either the Ferrari 488 GT or the Ford GT which dominated Le Mans, and both marques will use the same BoP settings issued just before the Le Mans 24 Hours. The Ford and Ferrari will race at 1248kg and 1268kg respectively.

Chapter 17
Epilogue II

IT'S 92 DEGREES IN THE SHADE AND, on the blacktop parking lot adjacent to the Ford Product Development Center in Dearborn in mid-July, there ain't much in the way of shade. But that hasn't deterred upwards of 3500 employees from gathering to celebrate Ford's victory in the 24 Hours of Le Mans—along with the news that Ford had officially extended its commitment to race the Ford GT in IMSA, the WEC and Le Mans through the end of the 2019 season.

It was considerably cooler late the previous night, when for the first time since 1966, the office lights in Ford's World Headquarters at 1 American Road were lit to read GT WINS AT LE MANS…and three young men from Wilton, California, Tägerwilen, Germany and Le Mans, France, shared a few joyous, carefree moments posing for photos in front of the rare display of corporate pride. The trio had been about to leave when a car pulled up to the curb and a young couple and their little boy disembarked to take-in the scene. After chatting about the GT WINS AT LE MANS light show with the Californian and explaining that her son watches Steve McQueen's epic movie *Le Mans* on a weekly basis, the woman asked "Do you work for Ford?"

Ten minutes and a dozen phone camera images later (by celebrated photographer Mike "Ansel" O'Gara) the family departed with memories of a lifetime and Joey Hand, Dirk Müller, Sebastien Bourdais and O'Gara headed back to The Henry Ford hotel to prepare for the morrow's victory celebration.

The following day, after a guided tour of the Henry Ford

automotive museum at Greenfield Village, they joined Ryan Briscoe, Richard Westbrook, Chip Ganassi, Rob Kauffman, Mike Hull, O'Gara and some of the key players at Ford including Fields, Nair, Pericak, Rushbrook and Henry Ford III for a meet 'n greet with Ford employees at the lunchtime celebration in the parking lot.

After some opening remarks by Master of Ceremonies, noted raconteur (and Motorsport Hall of Fame race driver) Tom Kendall, Bill Ford, executive chairman of the Ford Motor Company stepped to the microphone.

"I've had some amazing moments in my lifetime, and some incredible moments in my career," he said. "But very few will ever top standing on that podium with the national anthem being played. It was incredible. I'm not ashamed to tell you I had tears in my eyes…and that was before Sebastien Bourdais gave me a full frontal with the champagne!

"Standing there I thought about everything that had come before me. I thought about 50 years ago when my uncle, Henry Ford II decided to take on Ferrari and go to Le Mans and win… Then I was with my cousin Edsel who was there in '66 when we won, and to have him there again this year was incredible,

Tom Kendall regales a Who's Who of the Le Mans-winning team.

because he is the only person still at Ford to really play a major part in both those victories.

"I was thinking about my uncle Henry, and I was thinking about my father who took me Indianapolis every year as a child. I wish that both my father and my uncle could have been on there on the podium at Le Mans with me, to see what we had done again as Ford Motor Company.

"So I just want to say to each and every one of you: Thank You."

Ford was followed to the microphone by Mark Fields, President and CEO of the Ford Motor Company.

"I want to tell you a quick story," he said, "When we were originally thinking about developing the GT, the first proposal from Raj and the team was what I would call a souped-up Mustang they wanted to race in the GT series. And I said: 'Can we win?' They said, 'Well we think we can be OK and be competitive.' And then we agreed, 'You know what? If we're gonna go somewhere, we play to win: we don't just play to play.'

"And they came back with what you see today…and I have to tell you, sitting in the pits with Chip and the rest of the gang, and that car coming across, it was history in the making and this is what makes our company so special: we have a heritage which, for me, heritage is history with a future.

"This shows us as a company, whether it's racing or competing in the marketplace or giving back to community… you name it: When we come together and we set a winning aspiration, we can achieve anything."

Fields was followed by Nair, arm in cast.

"I've been telling people that I hurt my elbow racing at Le Mans. That sounds really sexy until you realize what really happened was that I fell off the pit wall prior to the race," he laughed.

"Obviously, it's an honor for me to be here today to celebrate the success we had with the win at Le Mans with the Ford GT program. The one thing I'd want to emphasize is that we've had a fantastic team between Ford and all of our partners. We were just blessed to have this great group of people, this team that gave up so many nights and weekends and holidays to make it all happen. Also, to do that while we were developing the production car at the same time is just an amazing accomplishment, and I'm just personally grateful for the total team effort in making that happen.

"I'm pleased to say that it doesn't end here. This is not just a one win and leave. We've announced that we're going to keep racing the GT all the way through the 2019 season.

"So we're not done. Our next step on both sides of the ocean is an IMSA championship and a WEC championship, and so we're gonna focus on that and then be back here with another Le Mans win. I don't make promises; other people do that for me. But we're going to do our best!"

Dave Pericak was next up. And he began not by heaping praise on the men and women behind the 2016 Le Mans-winning effort, but by paying tribute to a number of gentlemen who were Ford's guests of honor at the ceremony, namely Joe Balcerowiak, Bob Corn, Jim Johnson, Hank Lenox, Joe Macura, Larry Nemshick, Gus Scussel, Jerry Stoll, Jerry Schly and Mose Nowland, all of whom were part of Ford's engineering and engine development group on the 1966 Le Mans program.

Next, Pericak invited Nowland up to the dais for a special presentation: a framed French flag. But not just any framed French flag. It was the *drapeau tricolore* Nowland purloined off

Mose Nowland with his souvenir of the 1966 (and 2016) 24 Hours of Le Mans.

the pit roof shortly after Ford's 1-2-3 finish in 1966. The flag had been in his basement all the years since, until he presented it to Ford in the weeks just before the 2016 race.

"I'd been in racing with Ford for 23 years," Nowland said, "and I'd never picked up a souvenir. Well, when our cars finished 1-2-3 and all the champagne corks were popping, I thought I'd get myself a little souvenir.

"On top of each light post along pit lane, there was a French flag. So I stacked a couple of barrels on top of one another, very carefully climbed on top and took down the flag above our pit. A couple of guys started yelling, but I jumped down, ducked into the crowd and got away.

"I treated the flag honorably. The first chance I got I folded it nicely, then put it in my suitcase for the flight home and it's been in my basement ever since.

"I got it out a few months ago and saw that it was in reasonably good shape, so I called Ford to see if they wanted to take it with them to Le Mans this year. I don't know if it was a good luck charm, but it certainly didn't hurt!

"I told Dave Pericak he's welcome to take it again next year..."

But as Nair said, before worrying about Le Mans circa 2017, there was the matter of winning the IMSA and WEC championships. Thanks to a heroic effort, Ford Chip Ganassi Racing had already backed up its Le Mans win with an impressive one-two finish at the 6 Hours of Watkins Glen—this after having had to prepare their two Ford GTs for overseas transport to the United States and repacking their shipping crates within little more than 24 hours of the finish of the 24 Hours of Le Mans. Then it was back to Indianapolis via Paris by trains, planes and/or automobiles where they had a week to rebuild the race cars (including re-installing the IMSA data collection equipment) in time to load them on the transporters for the trip to upstate New York.

Just days after Westbrook and Briscoe scored their second IMSA win in succession—with Hand and Müller finishing second—it was off to Canadian Tire Motorsports Park (aka Mosport) near Toronto; but not before IMSA implemented the most significant BoP adjustments of the season.

While the minimum weight for the Corvette C7.R and Porsche 911 RSR was lowered by 10 kilos (22 pounds), the Ford GT's minimum weight was raised by 15 kilos (33 pounds)—

It's hard to top 1-3-4 at Le Mans but 1-2 at Watkins Glen came close.

for those keeping score at home, a 25 kilo/55 pound swing. Additionally the Corvette received an increase in power and torque via wider air restrictors while the Ford GT lost power and torque due to turbo boost restrictions across virtually the entire operational range of the EcoBoost V6.

Unsurprisingly, the Magnussen/Garcia Corvette won the pole in Canada only for Westbrook and Briscoe to come out on top in the race when Goldberg rolled the dice on the #67 Ford GT's final pit stop, opting for fuel only to gain track position. On a circuit where overtaking an equally matched car is all but impossible—and the Michelins stood-up to a double stint—Briscoe cruised to a relatively easy victory.

Leaving Canada for a well-earned rest, the IMSA standings read Corvette's Oliver Gavin and Tommy Milner 192, Westbrook and Briscoe 187.

However, the next event at Lime Rock Park saw Ford's win streak halted at three. Westbrook's pole-winning car was shuffled off the course on the opening lap, with Gavin and Milner coming through ahead of Magnussen and Garcia to score Corvette's 100th GT win in IMSA competition. Westbrook and

Corvette won the pole but Ford had the last laugh at Mosport.

Briscoe were forced to settle for third while Hand and Müller finished fifth.

The team arrived in Elkhart Lake, Wsconsin and the Continental Road Race Showcase at Road America with sad hearts, having learned that Chris Amon had passed away after a long battle with cancer. Speaking on behalf of the Ford Motor Company, Edsel B. Ford II said, "All of us at Ford are sad to learn of the passing of Chris Amon. Chris was a true gentleman, on and off the track, and I treasured my friendship with him over these past several years.

"Although Chris was not well enough to attend Le Mans this year, we were pleased to have his son Alex with us. I know Chris was following with great interest our victory that day. Our condolences to his family, friends and fans from around the world."

The Road America race was Hand's and Müller's to lose after taking the pole position. But a bent tie rod thought to have been damaged in a "hard landing" when the car came down off the air jacks (at least that was Müller's story and he was sticking to it) cost them three laps, leaving Westbrook and Briscoe to carry the Ford banner. They duly carried it into the lead before an overly optimistic passing attempt by Porsche's Nick Tandy resulted in a three-way collision with Westbrook and Fisichella's Ferrari, paving the way for Milner to jump from fifth to first in the final laps, with a disappointed Westbrook second.

Hand and Müller led the Ford charge at a sultry Virginia International Raceway in late August, coming home runner-up to the Magnussen/Garcia Corvette while Westbrook and Briscoe were fortunate to garner points for fourth. A bold gamble on tire selection in qualifying backfired, and they opted to start at the very back of the GT field (behind the GTLM and GTD cars) on a new set of Michelins. But Westbrook and Briscoe had only managed to climb to sixth place when, first, Gavin crashed his Corvette and, on the subsequent restart, Bamber's Porsche unceremoniously punted Fisichella into the Virgina countryside, promoting the #67 Ford GT to fourth place. The net result left Gavin and Milner (287) in the GTLM lead by just seven points over Westbrook and Briscoe with two races remaining.

Meanwhile, the WEC team had its first post-Le Mans outing at the 6 Hours of Nürburgring where, with Johnson "re-assigned" as planned to Multimatic's IMSA Continental Tires SportsCar Championship effort with Maxwell, Mücke and Pla went it alone in the #66 Ford GT with Franchitti, Priaulx and

Hand and Müller chased Corvette home at VIR.

Tincknell continuing in the sister car.

Mücke snagged first place on the opening lap only to fall to third when the #97 Aston Martin barged past into the lead. Tincknell circulated in fifth through the early laps before a fire erupted during the first pit stop when a fuel valve stuck open moments after he handed the car over to Priaulx. Although the conflagration was eventually extinguished, Priaulx was more than 20 laps down when he rejoined. The #66 continued running third until the in-car camera caught Mücke undoing his seat belts while rolling down pit lane as he prepared to hand over to Pla. The subsequent drive-through penalty dropped them to a fourth-place finish.

Six weeks later the WEC traveled to the rarefied air of Mexico City. With the Ford GTs struggling to generate heat in their tires on the Autodromo Hermanos Rodriguez' ultra-smooth surface, FCGR qualified sixth and seventh in the seven-car GTE-Pro field. After making a great start, Pla was belted off the track by one of the Ferraris—with no penalty assessed—only to be penalized

196

The Mexican skies threatened but failed to deliver.

himself later after a coming-together with one of the Aston Martins. In contrast, Tincknell, Priaulx and Franchitti ran in the top three before changing to Michelin wets under threatening skies. When the expected downpour failed to materialize, the #67 Ford GT was consigned to an unrepresentative fifth-place finish.

"Fifth truly is poor reward for the effort we had this weekend," said Priaulx. "Although we didn't have the ultimate pace to challenge for the win, as a team we ran a flawles s race. We got a little unlucky with the poor conditions, or I should say we got a little unlucky when the conditions didn't deteriorate as we expected. But our execution was flawless and I really belive if we can continue to perform as we did this weekend we'll be successful."

The less said about the Lone Star Grand Prix weekend WEC/IMSA doubleheader at Circuit of the Americas in mid-September the better. Check that: Maxwell extended his Continental Tire SportsCar series record for pole positions to 15. The following day he and Johnson clinched the IMSA Continental Tire SportsCar Challenge drivers and team titles with a victory on Friday in what the Blue Oval contingent hoped was the first of a three-race sweep. But after capturing the IMSA pole, Briscoe

The IMSA and WEC races at CotA mirrored another.

was pushed down the order on the opening lap, while Müller was drilled from behind by a BMW and completed the opening tour a half lap down to the field. Later, Briscoe and Gavin made contact while disputing fifth spot, resulting in a broken steering arm on the Ford and, ultimately, leading to a ninth-place finish with Hand and Müller finishing P6 after being off the pace throughout the weekend.

Things were little better on the WEC side, where the air conditioning had failed on the #66 Ford GT in the opening laps, resulting in a 20-minute stay in the garage effecting repairs. Later, an impatient LMP2 competitor punted Mücke into the gravel, the net result being the battered car eventually trailed home 19 laps down to the victorious Aston Martin of Thim and Sorenson. Meanwhile the pace of the Ferraris and Aston Martins left Franchitti, Priaulx and Tincknell little chance of making the podium. Although Priaulx made a heroic effort to wrest third place from the AF Corse Ferrari in the closing laps, he came up 13 seconds short. Thus the Ford GT score on the weekend read: P4 and P7 in WEC, P6 and P9 in IMSA.

In the bigger picture, although Franchitti, Priaulx and Tincknell regained the top ten in the WEC LMGTE Pro drivers standings, with rounds remaining at Fuji, Bahrain and Shanghai, Mücke and Pla were all but eliminated in their bid for an FIA Endurance Cup for Drivers title; likewise the results ended any hopes Ford and FCGR had of claiming the FIA Endurance Trophy for LMGTE Pro Teams and for Manufacturers. Similarly, Corvette virtually clinched the IMSA Weathertech SportsCar Championship's manufacturers crown in the Lone Star state. However, while long shots, the IMSA team and drivers championships (for Briscoe and Westbrook) were more than just mathematical possibilities heading to the Petit Le Mans season finale.

So though they would have switched roles with Gavin, Milner and Corvette in a heartbeat, FCGR arrived at Road Atlanta with a clear mandate.

"We have to win," said Hull. "That's our entire focus: Control what's within our power; win and then let other people tell us what it means as far as the championship."

Qualifying was a case of mission accomplished. Hours after Maxwell and Johnson clinched the Continental Tire Challenge's Grand Sport manufacturers title for Ford with their sixth win of the season, Westbrook planted the #67 Ford on pole ahead of the Magnussen/Garcia/Mike Rockenfeller Corvette and the Risi Ferrari. Hand posted fourth-best time ahead of the Scuderia Corse Ferrari and the quickest of the Rahal Letterman Lanigan BMWs, while the Gavin/Milner/Marcel Fassler Corvette languished in seventh.

Better yet, Westbrook jumped into the early lead and pulled to a seven-second advantage over Garcia and the two Ferraris with Hand in fifth ahead of the Gavin/Milner/Fassler Corvette. But after a jammed wheel nut on the first pit stop dropped the #67 Ford GT down the order, Westbrook tried a low-percentage pass on Jonathan Edwards' BMW, which had just exited the pits on cold tires. Not only was Westbrook penalized for the resulting "avoidable contact," one of the Ford's intercooler pipes was damaged in the mixup, necessitating lengthy repairs and ending all hope of a team or a drivers championship.

Nevertheless, Hand, Müller and Bourdais were in the hunt, chasing the leading Risi Ferrari most of the way. Hennek's gamble—changing left-side tires only on the final stop—vaulted the #67 Ford GT into first place. But Risi Competizione had

Time expired on FCGR's bid for the IMSA championship.

the upper hand in this "Le Mans" and, 14 laps later, the scarlet Ferrari regained a lead it would hold to the finish as Hand fended-off the championship-winners' fast-closing Corvette for second place in the final laps.

The space beneath the FCGR transporters awning was a very, very different place following the 2016 IMSA season finale than it had been at the conclusion of the 2015 campaign—and not just because the 19th edition of Petit Le Mans took place under an October sky that might have been dialed-up by the local Chamber of Commerce rather than some demented soul bent on reliving the Life of Noah.

A year ago the mood was a mixture of anticipation, pride and no small degree of trepidation as the Ford family, executives of the Ford Motor Company and the management, crew and at least one driver at Ford Chip Ganassi Racing embarked on an audacious program to develop a new and unproven race car into a winning proposition in the world's most unforgiving contest of endurance. Now, 363 days—and nights—later, many of those same people gathered under the FCGR awning in a shared sense of camaraderie and accomplishment, if ever so slightly

The FCGR Fords dominated the 6 Hours of Fuji.

shadowed by the scuttling of their championship hopes that afternoon. Make no mistake however, the prevailing mood was one of mutual satisfaction and commitment: satisfaction in a job well done; commitment to finishing the job of winning championships and more races in the future.

Indeed, FCGR delivered on the latter front with a resounding 1-2 finish in the 6 Hours of Fuji in mid-October. Having earlier pared down the lineup on the #67 to a Priaulx/Tincknell partnership, the WEC squad dominated practice and qualifying with one or the other of the Ford GTs setting the pace in each of the three free practices before Mücke and Pla grabbed the team's first pole position. What's more, Priaulx and Tincknell made it an all-Ford front row while the Rigon/Bird Ferrari was third, more than 0.4 seconds off the pole.

Tincknell got the best of Pla at the green flag to snatch the lead into the first turn. The Fords then ran in close formation for most of the race, the only hiccups coming when Tincknell had a minor coming-together with a GTE-Am Porsche and when Pla indulged in a quick but harmless spin. Six hours and 54 seconds after the start, the #67 Ford GT took FCGR's first WEC checkered flag with the #66 coming home some 14 seconds behind, but the best part of half a minute clear of the third-placed Bruni/Colado Ferrari.

Fortune finally smiled on the WEC team in the Land of the Rising Sun.

"Today's result was great for Ford, for the team, for Multimatic and for Chip Ganassi. It's a young team, it's a new team and today they were faultless," said Priaulx, with a nod toward his post-Mexico City comments. "The pit stops were brilliant, Harry (Tincknell) did a great job and I'm delighted we finally got our first win. We've had some really good performances this year but we haven't had the result we all deserve. This one is for the team."

"This is a fabulous result after quite a long dry spell, so to then get a 1-2 is a great tribute to the hard work of all four drivers, the team and to the support we receive from the Ford team around the world," said Howard-Chappell. "It's a great result, a great lift and it helps us in the championship."

The Fuji triumph not only boded well for the remaining two races in the 2016 WEC season, but for next year's IMSA and WEC campaigns, especially the 24 Hours of Le Mans. After all, 2017 marks another important milestone for Ford: The 50th anniversary of their 1967 Le Mans "All American" triumph with A.J. Foyt, Dan Gurney and the Ford GT Mk IV.

Acknowledgments

Were I to name everyone whose support, advice and insight went into this project, I'd have to add a third and maybe even a fourth epilogue. However, I would be grossly remiss were I not to express my heartfelt thanks to Chip Ganassi for making this adventure possible. As I said about a year ago, Nelson Ledges to Le Mans: Not bad for a couple of guys from Pittsburgh.

Thanks as well as to everyone at Ford Chip Ganassi Racing including Mike Hull, Mike O'Gara, Grant Weaver, Mel Harder, John Olguin, Brad Zimmerman, Kelby Krauss, Shannon Logan, Brad Goldberg, John Hennek and, especially, Brett Knostman, Tyler Rees and their tireless crews for putting up with me. Likewise, heartfelt appreciation to Larry Holt, George Howard-Chappell, Charlie Cadieux, Julian Sole, Peter Gibbons, Carol Melville and their colleagues at Multimatic. And of course, to many kind people named Ford – Bill, Edsel and Henry – as well as Raj Nair, Dave Pericak, Mark Rushbrook, Kevin Groot, John Kipf, Jay Ward, Lindsay Morle and my old pal Bernie Marcus, along with Kevin Kennedy and Lachelle Laney at Campbell & Company, EMC's John Love and Paul Ryan, IMSA's Nate Siebens, Corvette's Ryan Smith, Barbara Burns of Risi Competizione and Jean Reisterer and Todd English at Roush Yates Engines.

I am also eternally grateful to iRacing.com for affording me the luxury and flexibility of pursuing this undertaking. I don't say iRacing is the world's premier online motorsports simulation service because I work there; I work there because iRacing is the world's premier online motorsports simulation service.

On a more personal note, thanks to motorsports' premier editor/wordsmith John Zimmermann for all your efforts and to Jeff Eddings, John Glang, Angelo Horse, Wolfgang Hustedt, Dennis Molnar, Eunice Nasri, Paul Pfanner, Steve Potter, Corrine Vitolo, Brian Wagner and a passel of people named Novario, Gutowski, Gallagher, Nixon, Schaeffer, Snodgrass, Aber, Jordan, Saville and Teague for your support through harrowing times. But especially to Laura for the joy and poetry you bestow on our family and to Matthew – always the iconoclast, ever the strong, creative, devoted son.

David Phillips

David Phillips spent more than two decades as a freelance journalist covering Indy and sports car racing for some of the world's leading motorsports publications including *Racer*, *Autoweek*, *Motoring News*, *Motor Sport*, *Autosport*, *IndyCar*, *Auto Action*, *Sports Car* and *On Track* as well as *racer.com*, *speed.com*, *USA Today* and the *Pittsburgh Post-Gazette*. Since 2009 he has been publications director of *iRacing.com*, the world's premier online motorsports simulation service.